Father M. Eugene Boylan

THE PRIEST'S WAY TO GOD

THE PRIEST'S WAY TO GOD

BY

FATHER M. EUGENE BOYLAN O.C.S.O.
Abbot of Mount St. Joseph, Roscrea

AUTHOR OF

This Tremendous Lover

AND

Difficulties in Mental Prayer

THE NEWMAN PRESS
WESTMINSTER, MARYLAND
1962

First impression June 1962

Second impression October 1962

Library of Congress Card Number: 62-17187

© SCEPTER PUBLISHERS LIMITED,
DUBLIN 1962

PRINTED AND BOUND IN THE REPUBLIC OF IRELAND
BY O'GORMAN LTD., GALWAY.

NIHIL OBSTAT: THOMAS F. O'REILLY, CENSOR THEOL.
IMPRIMI POTEST: ✠ JOANNES CAROLUS, ARCHIEP.
DUBLINEN., HIBERNIAE PRIMAS. DUBLINI DIE 11 OCT.
1962

59743

CONTENTS

FOREWORD

THE life of the diocesan priest is so difficult—it is perhaps the most difficult of all lives in the Church—that any attempt to help him, no matter how inadequate, needs no justification. So I make no apology for publishing a second collection of notes on a subject which I have already discussed in *The Spiritual Life of the Priest*. The matter of these notes is not new to the readers of *Pagan Missions*, and it is due to the kindness of the Editor of that journal that I am able to compile these pages. It is not the only kindness for which I have to thank him.

Despite the high holiness to which a priest is called and the eminent sanctity of the office which he fulfills, his life has to be lived amidst all the difficulties of the world without the protection and the preparation that is usually given to religious who, as such, are merely bound to tend to perfection. The diocesan priest therefore deserves every help that can be given to him to live that life of perfection which his office demands from him. Where is he to look for help?

To anticipate the final answer to this question, we may remind him of God's assurance to the great apostle: 'Paul, my grace is sufficient for thee'. 'The spirit of holiness', conferred on him in ordination by the very words of the Sacrament, assures him of this continual grace of God. And, in passing, let us remember that the word grace implies something given beyond merit, or even without merit. It is gratuitous. One could truly rewrite the text: 'Paul, my mercy is sufficient for thee. My goodness is sufficient for thee!' And it might be well to repeat it with a new accent: 'Paul, *My* goodness is sufficient for thee—do not worry about your own lack of goodness!' This seems too good to be true. But that is the great truth—that no man has even conceived the things God has prepared for those who love him. We are dealing with infinite Goodness, and only infinite Truth can give it adequate expression.

We can find in our Mass a reminder of these infinities with which we are dealing. The Mass is a sacrifice, and every sacrifice involves the offering of a gift to God by which the offerer signifies the interior gift which he makes of himself to God. At the offertory of each Mass, —without claiming that this is the theological or liturgical interpretation of that ceremony—we can imagine the Church attempting to offer herself to God by the offering of the bread and the wine. It must be realised however that here we are trying to conceive the Church without Christ, but including everyone else—the souls in purgatory, the whole Church on earth, all the Saints in heaven, and the Queen of Saints as well. We can imagine that Christ looks at this offering, and says: 'It is good—but it is not good enough for my Father'. And so he changes the bread and wine into his own sacrifice, and comes down from the Altar to change the members of the Church into himself by Holy Communion. This is obviously not the theological interpretation of the liturgy, but it corresponds to a most important truth which seems to underlie all God's dealings with the world which he created, and of which we can remind ourselves at every Mass,—the truth that 'only Christ is good enough for God'.

This seems to be in harmony with the fact that, in

the very moment when God created man, he raised him up to a participation in his own divine nature by supernatural grace. It seems to be the reason why, when the sin of Adam upset his plan, he decided to restore all things in Christ. It seems to be the reason why Christ became man, why he instituted the sacraments by which he could reach out throughout time and space to enter into and to live in every human soul, sharing every lawful human activity. For that is obviously the plan of God; and it is in the carrying out of this plan that we priests are called to co-operate. St. Pius X was quite definite in stating that this is our work; he was equally definite in stating that the first step in this work is to form Christ in ourselves. The reason is obvious. Not merely is it true that only Christ is good enough for God; it is also true that only Christ is good enough for God's work. 'Without me', he said, 'you can do nothing'. We priests fail completely in our vocation if we fail to put on Christ, if we attempt to do the work of Christ by human strength alone.

On the other hand, in Christ we have an adequate means of giving God his due. All statements in human words about God are under-statements. But perhaps the greatest understatement is that made by God himself: 'This is my beloved son in whom I am well pleased'. We are here given a glimpse of the ineffable joy and complete satisfaction which the Father finds in his Son, who is all that God can desire for himself since the Son, too, is God. Even after becoming man, he is still God and perfectly pleasing to the Father. Even when as a man, he has associated himself with us, taking on himself the burden of all our sins and exposing himself to the Divine Justice, he is still infinitely pleasing to God, especially in his supreme Sacrifice on the Cross.

It is this same sacrifice which we offer in every Mass. It is the prayer of this same 'well-pleasing' son which we offer every time we recite our breviary. It is the power of this same Son which is always with us in his work, and it is the merits of this same Son, and the infinite mercy of his Father, which give us reason for unlimited confidence.

It is in the hope that what we have written will help priests to remove the obstacles to union with Christ, and to develop that union as Christ wishes it to be developed, that we publish these pages. May Mary, the Mother of Christ, who is so powerful to unite men with Christ, make us one with him, as he has prayed and suffered and died to make us one.

Fr. M. Eugene Boylan O.C.S.O.

Mount St. Joseph Abbey,
Roscrea, Ireland.
24th October 1961

CHAPTER ONE

PERFECTION IN THE PRIESTHOOD

BEFORE we discuss the spiritual life of a priest—and particularly his life of prayer—we must first get rid of any misunderstanding about the perfection to which he is called. There is such a close connection between prayer and perfection that any error about the latter will lead to a wrong standard for the former. St. Thomas did not regard the priesthood as a state of perfection; he did, however, describe the episcopate and the religious life as states of perfection. As a result there is a vague feeling, which may unconsciously lower one's standards, that a priest, as a priest, is not called to the same perfection of life as, say, a religious. This is completely wrong.

There is no need to discuss the question whether changes subsequent to the time of St. Thomas would have caused him to alter his view of the priesthood as a state of life. The obligation of a priest to be perfect has other sources. It arises from his very office, and by that office he is placed under an obligation that is not only different from, but much superior to, that of a religious. A religious is bound to tend to perfection, and his state of life is excellently designed to help him to do so. But a priest, as Cardinal Manning says, is ordained to exercise perfection. He must be holy before ordination.

His obligation as a priest is to *be* holy; the obligation to *acquire* holiness only arises through a lack of the holiness that is demanded by his office.

Since St. Thomas is quoted in this discussion, let us hear his views on the perfection of the priest in comparison with that of a religious. He deals with the objection that one should be perfect before undertaking the obligations of the religious just as the walls of a building should be dried before the weight of the roof is laid upon them, and he replies: 'Sicut supra dictum est, ordines sacri praexigunt sanctitatem; sed status religionis est exercitium quoddam ad sanctitatem assequendum. Unde pondus ordinum imponendum est parietibus jam per sanctitatem desiccatis sed pondus religionis dessicat parietes, id est homines ab humore vitiorum.'[1] And the previous statement to which he refers is quite definitive for our purpose, for he writes: 'Per sacrum ordinem aliquis deputatur ad dignissima ministeria, quibus ipsi Christo servitur in sacramento altaris, ad quod requiritur major sanctitas interior, quam requirat etiam religionis status.'[2]

This is quite conclusive. The misunderstanding arises from the fact that St. Thomas was rather considering the question of the priesthood as a stable *state*; and, as he knew it, the state of religion was more stable. Readers will find an excellent discussion of the question in Dr. Mahoney's book, *The Secular Priesthood*.

It is unfortunate that many manuals of moral theology are quite inadequate and sometimes inaccurate on the point. It is not for the present writer to quarrel with the standard works of theologians, but the following phrase in Ferreres' *Compendium Theologiae Moralis* seems unfortunate. In the introduction to Tract X, *de Statu religioso*, the learned author writes: 'Status sacerdotalis, licet dignitate omnium praestantissimum sit, ratione tamen perfectionis longe vitae religiosae cedit.' If the author is speaking of the priesthood as a *state*, he is, no doubt, technically correct.[3] If he means to suggest that a 'secular' priest is called to a lesser degree of perfection than a religious, as such (e.g. a lay brother), the best comment is that of Cardinal Manning: 'In my belief that proposition is erroneous and offensive to pious ears and injurious to our Divine Master and to the Holy Ghost.'[4]

Whatever about his state, his office demands personal holiness in the priest. It is not merely a question of dignity, or of external holiness (if there be such a thing!). The text of St. Thomas is quite clear; he speaks of interior holiness. That such is required is evident from the fact that a priest's primary function is to offer sacrifice. This sacrifice, in so far as it is a personal act, is a lie if his heart is not in accord with his actions. To avoid further discussion here, let it suffice to quote Pius X, whose *Letter to Catholic Priests* should be read and re-read by every priest and student.

The Holy Father writes: 'If such sanctity was demanded in the Old Law from a priesthood which was but a type and a figure, what shall be demanded from us, the victim of whose sacrifice is Christ? . . . There are some who think and teach that the whole value of a priest consists in the fact that he devotes himself to the needs of others. How fallacious and disastrous is such a doctrine. Personal sanctity alone will make us the kind of men demanded by our divine vocation— men crucified to the world, men to whom the things of the world are dead, men walking in newness of life.'[5]

One cannot too often turn to the extraordinary words addressed by our Lord to his Apostles, on the eve of his death, when he was ordaining them priests. 'I am the true vine . . . Abide in me: and I in you. As the branch cannot bear fruit of itself, unless it abide in the vine, so neither can you, unless you abide in me. I am the vine; you the branches: he that abideth in me and I in him, the same beareth much fruit: for without me you can do nothing.'[6] Thus, on an occasion when his words must be taken as specially significant, in a matter that was intimately connected with his life-work and with the purpose of his death, our Lord laid it down that not only was union with him the way to fruitfulness in the ministry, but that there was no other way. In fact, he stated that 'if any one abide not in me: he shall be cast forth as a branch, and shall wither.'[7] No priest, then, can set aside union with our Lord—intimate and complete union with our Lord—as something outside his vocation, something peculiarly the vocation of religious. *Absit!* A priest, as a priest, is called to the highest perfection. He is in a class apart. While the religious must tend to holiness, the priest must be holy.

This should be a source of great confidence to every priest. No one will deny that the life many priests have to live presents not a few difficulties and obstacles to holiness. Yet, since it is obligatory, holiness must be possible. Since holiness is an essential duty of his office, the priest can be certain that all the necessary graces are available. The character of the priesthood received in Holy Orders—that mysterious participation in the priesthood of Jesus Christ—is the promise and the pledge of all graces needed for our priesthood. St. Thomas would even call the character a 'cause' of grace.[8] By ordination a special relation is set up between the soul and the Holy Ghost; on him, who is God himself and who is our sanctifier, we can rely for all that our priesthood entails. Our Lord himself has exhorted us: 'Have confidence, I have overcome the world.'[9] So that even if our lives in the world are fraught with difficulty, we can be absolutely certain of his omnipotent aid. In all these things we can overcome 'because of him that hath loved us'; in all things we are made rich in him, so that nothing can be wanting to us in any grace. With St. Peter let each of us launch out into the deep at the word of the Master, confident of a full draught; with St. Paul let each of us say: 'I know whom I have believed and I am certain that he is able to keep that which I have committed unto him.'[10]

The first difficulty about a priest's prayer—namely the feeling that he is not called to a high spirituality, that this is something reserved for religious, to which he need not, or even should not, aspire—is thereby removed. A priest must sum up in himself all the different types of the spiritual life, 'eminently' of course. He must be a contemplative, if his activity is to be fruitful. There is no other way for him. His vocation demands all the holiness of any religious order, even though it does not provide the same means to achieve it, and even though it may not—perhaps—have the same stability of organization that would make it technically a 'state.'[11]

Readers will forgive us for stressing this. It is true that many workers in the mission fields are religious. Even for these, we would stress the obligation to holiness which arises out of their priesthood. The reason is that in the missions regular religious life has often to be modified considerably, if not at times almost completely abandoned, so that the religious is no better off in respect of safeguards and assistance than the diocesan priest. He may, therefore, be tempted to feel that he is no longer obliged to acquire and to possess that holiness that would be his aim and his vocation in a more sheltered and regular observance. This would be a fatal error. As if St. Peter and St. Paul were saints only *in spite of* their apostolic vocation! Such religious are, as priests, called to the highest holiness, and as priests, in the exercise of their priesthood, can and must find the means to achieve it. They must school themselves from the very beginning to seek such means even in walks of life which render regular religious observance impossible. They have by ordination at least a title to, if not the actual possession of, all the graces necessary for holiness. But they must use those graces. That is where a religious can fail. He may have come to rely on his rule and regular life to bring him to perfection. Once the rule has to be modified by the needs of the mission-fields, and regular life becomes a dream never to be realized, there is a danger that he may give up hope of perfection, fail to take things energetically into his own hands and use the grace that is in him to be holy.

Our primary purpose in these pages is to discuss mental prayer for priests. But it is necessary to discuss these other matters to get things into their true perspective. Prayer is, of course, only a part of the spiritual life, yet it is a part that depends on, and gives expression to, the whole spiritual life. If any part of our spiritual life is defective, our prayer will be influenced by that defect—especially by a mistaken view of our vocation to holiness.

Another point which we should like to stress is this. Union with God is frequently put forward as the goal of prayer—a goal to which a man may attain after long years of prayer, penance and faithful service. Divine union would, then, be the end of a life of prayer in a chronological sense as well as a philosophic one. Such a view—while true in a way—could easily mislead us. For in a very important sense, divine union is the beginning of prayer—its 'principle', chronologically as well as philosophically. It is true a sinner can pray, but he must have at least that momentary union with God that is the result of actual grace. Prayer is a supernatural act, something superhuman, and therefore utterly impossible without God. Therefore from the very beginning we must see divine union as the foundation of our prayer. We pray not in order to achieve divine union—we achieved that in Baptism—but to develop it. Let us again refer to our Lord's words at the Last Supper; they must never be forgotten by the priest. 'Abide in me . . . without me you can do nothing.' That is the secret of how to pray; it is the secret of how to preach; it is the secret of how to be apostles; it is the secret of how to be saints. And there is no other way!

The pattern set by the Church in the breviary is highly significant. Each hour begins by a communing with God. 'Deus in adjutorium meum intende. Domine ad adjuvandum me festina.' That is the way we must approach all prayer. We must stir up the grace that is in us, by the imposition of hands. All we need is already ours, by the title of five sacraments. And also, may we add, by the title of our own poverty. '*Modicae fidei*'; why do we doubt? Let us pray in faith, nothing wavering. 'We know in whom we have confidence.' We have received the Holy Spirit, for our use. He it is who prayeth in us. All we have to do is to unite ourselves to him.

Before leaving this point, may we anticipate some later discussions, and draw the reader's attention to the need for faith—especially for faith in the powers given to our own souls by the sacraments we have received? We must believe in our power to pray, as we believe in our power to consecrate and to absolve. In fact we shall frequently be *forced* to *believe* in our capacity for prayer, for neither the prayer nor the power to pray will be at all in evidence. Yet we are participators in the priesthood of Christ. That will suffice—if we have faith in him.

Our spiritual life, then, from the very beginning is a life of union with God, which we have to develop. One of the principal ways of developing this life is prayer. How are we to go about it? To answer this question, it is again necessary to explain its perspective. There are three important things upon which our whole spiritual life depends, and which are so interconnected that no one of them can be discussed properly without reference to the others. These three are: spiritual reading, reflection and prayer. When we speak of prayer in these pages, we generally mean prayer in this sense, something distinct from our reading or reflection, and something which is of capital necessity for our advance in the spiritual life. The best way to describe what we mean is to make our own the words of St. Teresa: 'Mental prayer, in my opinion, is nothing else than being on terms of intimate friendship with God, frequently conversing in secret with him, who, we know, loves us.'[12] It is an elevation to God of our heart and soul, in which he is addressed, with or without words, in the second person singular. Using the term prayer in the sense which we have indicated, we do not consider thinking about God to be in itself prayer. It is of course often accompanied by a silent prayer of the heart; and it is one of the best ways to lead us to pray.

But it does not suffice, in itself, to satisfy the third need of the spiritual life we have indicated by the term prayer. We shall return to that point in a moment.

Before we go any further in this discussion, we have again to clear a way through the brambles and brushwood of misunderstanding. A distinction is made between vocal prayer and mental prayer. It is not for us to quarrel with traditional usage, but we may be permitted to deplore the effects arising from a misunderstanding of that distinction. Two particularly harmful notions can arise from it, and, in fact, have arisen. One is the idea that there is some type of vocal prayer which is not 'mental'; the other is that 'mental' prayer must never be made with words. It is hard to imagine any misunderstanding that can be more baneful to our spiritual life than these. There can obviously be no true prayer in which the mind does not in some way take part. And even the higher forms of contemplation may express themselves in words. Was St. Francis, who spent the night repeating 'My Lord and my God', not making 'mental prayer'?

Generally, the term vocal prayer is applied to that prayer wherein words are used and externally expressed, at least by lip-articulation; in most cases some ready-made formula is employed, for example the *Pater Noster* or the Psalms. One might say that in vocal prayer a person tries to conform his mind to a ready-made formula externally expressed, while in mental prayer, he starts with a 'meaning' and may try to express it in some way or other. Such a summing-up is quite inadequate, but it may help to get rid of the notion that the two things are mutually exclusive. One thing we insist upon: prayer does not cease to be mental prayer when one commences to use words, even if those words are borrowed ones, such as common aspirations or verses from the Psalms. The important point is not whether we express our meaning in words or acts, but whether we have a meaning to express, and also, indeed, whether we mean that meaning. Here we can certainly agree to a *caveat*. If you do use words in your mental prayer, be sure you mean what you say. It does not matter a whole lot whether you say what you mean: often, in fact, you will be quite incapable of saying it. Sometimes you can only 'babble.' These things don't matter; it is the 'meaning' that matters, in other words, the movements of the heart.

We also insist upon another point. Meditation, strictly so-called, in the sense of reflection, is not, as such, mental prayer, at least that mental prayer which we consider to be so essential for the spiritual life. Readers will forgive us if we are almost agressive on the point. We have met many souls who think and who, it would seem, were taught to think, that mental prayer consists essentially in 'consideration.' We do not, indeed, deny the need for consideration or reflection for the formation of convictions in the spiritual life. On the contrary, it is because we hold such to be so necessary that we are going to insist upon the importance of reading and reflection. But we are convinced that some more direct approach to God than that is necessary, and we feel that prayer is the time for that intimate approach. It is here that prayer can be defined as an elevation of the mind to God. One could, perhaps, argue that reflection is such an elevation and therefore a prayer. *Transeat!* We are not writing a theoretical treatise on the psychology and theologp of prayer; we are trying to draw up a programme of the exercises necessary for a priest who wishes to develop his spiritual life. If such meditation be prayer, such 'prayer' is, to our mind, not sufficient for a healthy spiritual life. Something more is needed and we reserve the term prayer for that something more.

However, we do not deny that there is a very common type of prayer in which the discursive operation of the intellect greatly predominates, leading, however, to some affections and to those acts of choice which are called resolutions. Indeed, it must be so for many people, if the 'meaning' we refer to above is to come into existence. But because of the misunderstanding of that unfortunate adjective 'mental', too many people consider that discursive meditation is the essential part of mental prayer. In fact, it is quite the other way about! The real prayer, the elevation of the mind and heart to God, is in the affections, in the movements of the will to God; the reflections, in themselves, are little more than a means to that end. It cannot be denied that in many cases the will is acting—we may say praying—even during the reflective part of the exercise. That, however, is *per accidens*. But in stressing the need for affections, what we wish to combat is the notion—by no means unheard-of—that mental prayer, properly so-called, ceases when the acts or affections commence, especially if these are made in words. As a matter of fact, it is only then that prayer in its fullness really commences. The whole purpose of meditation, in so far as it is connected with the exercise of prayer, is to get those acts going.

We shall have to postpone to our next chapter what we have to say about reading and reflection. The reader is probably impatient now, and wishes for something practical with regard to his mental prayer. To satisfy him, let us anticipate by a summary statement, which we shall develop and explain later. Once the current misunderstandings have been put aside and the initial novitiate completed, what one might call the 'technique' of prayer is comparatively simple. The whole thing can be summed up in this way. There is an exercise of private prayer, well-nigh essential for the spiritual life, which consists in talking to God, in one's own words, with or without words, according to one's inclination. The paradox is deliberate and is best elucidated by reminding the reader of the prayer to the Holy Ghost which begins, 'Deus cui omne cor patet, et omnis voluntas loquitur . . . ' Our wills can speak to God without words, and yet in the way indicated by the phrase, 'in our own words.' As a matter of practical policy, the use of words has nothing whatever to do with the nature of mental prayer. They are a means to an end, to be used if they help, to be omitted if they are a hindrance.

If it is as simple as all that, why do many men find it so hard? In practice, one answer to that question is another question, addressed to the individual priest who says he cannot pray. 'Do you do any regular spiritual reading'? That, to our mind, is the practical crux of the whole matter. In some ways we regard regular spiritual reading as more important than mental prayer itself, inasmuch as, if one looks after one's spiritual reading, mental prayer will look after itself.

To any priest who looks for guidance in the matter of his mental prayer, our reply is this. First of all, he must agree to a regular daily ration of spiritual reading. Given this, and provided we are not dealing with a beginner or with someone in unusual circumstances, to the ordinary priest who is living a 'good' life, we would say: Fix a time each day for your mental prayer.

Stand, sit or kneel as you find best. Start off by turning to God. After that, it does not matter much what happens, as long as you do not allow yourself to be deliberately distracted. When you find yourself distracted, and that will be often, turn gently back. Use a book if you wish, but don't turn the exercise into spiritual reading. Never strain yourself. All must be done gently. Do not be disappointed if you achieve nothing. Hold on. God will come in his own time.

This is a rather summary prescription which we intend to discuss at greater length in later chapters. But it provides, if not for the *melius esse* of prayer, at least for the *esse* of prayer as we believe it to be necessary. So essential do we consider some such effort at private prayer for the spiritual life of the priest that we would personally quite cheerfully take full responsibility for all the time that a priest prudently spends in such an exercise no matter how fruitful the time might actually have been if devoted to other good works. The apparent failure and fruitlessness of our effort must not lessen our determination to persevere in it. Very often God allows the fruit of our efforts to find him to appear only at some other moment of the day. Sometimes he wishes us to learn that, even though we must keep on making efforts, the result depends completely on him and his bounty. Accordingly, he withholds his graces for a time and then bestows them in such abundance, and so clearly out of all proportion to our own efforts, that they are unmistakably the result of his mercy rather than of our own merits. If we remember that in persevering in our attempts at prayer we are continually offering and giving ourselves to him, and if at the same time we regard everything that he gives to us as the gift of his mercy rather than as the reward of our merits, we shall enter into a new relationship with him full of a peace and confidence which no shortcomings on our own part can lessen. And while we must not lose sight of those shortcomings we must remember, too, that God has given us his Son for our Saviour so that nothing is wanting to us in any grace. Let us cast our burden on him . . . *Ipse faciet*.

[1] *Summa Theol.* II-IIae, q. 189 art. 1 ad 3
[2] Ibid., q. 184 art. 8
[3] Cf. Apost. Const. *Provida Mater Ecclesia*, Feb. 2nd 1947
[4] Purcell, *Life*, II, p. 764
[5] *Haerenti Animo*, Aug. 4th 1908: Cf. also A. A. S., IV. p. 1912
[6] John XV, 1-5
[7] Ibid.
[8] Cf. *Summa Theol.* III, q. 69 art. 10
[9] John XVI, 33
[10] 2 Tim. I, 12
[11] Cf., however, Mahoney, op. cit.
[12] *Autobiography*, Ch. VIII, 7

CHAPTER TWO

READING AND REFLECTION ·

In the last chapter we made an attempt to clear the ground before discussing mental prayer and its place in the life of a priest. We insisted that every priest is called to high holiness and that, therefore, the graces necessary to achieve such holiness must be available despite the handicaps that may arise from the circumstances of a priest's life. It is important to remember this vocation to holiness for there is a close connection between the prayer of a priest and his progress in the spiritual life; a duty to advance in holiness almost necessarily implies a duty to advance in mental prayer.

And yet, for more than a few priests, the whole subject of mental prayer is a problem. Many a fervent priest will tell you that his mental prayer is a burden, and that he performs it just as a duty, almost even as a penance. Some may question its usefulness; others find it so difficult that they may be tempted to give it up altogether. This is a state of things which calls for some explanation. It is true, of course, that mental prayer, like everything else worth while, is not altogether an easy thing. It demands an effort. But the intrinsic difficulties are by no means insuperable, and if so many priests find mental prayer hard, it is natural to ask whether there are extrinsic factors which contribute in no small way to the problem.

Such a factor, for instance, might be a misunderstanding of the techinque of prayer. In order to illustrate what we mean, let us take a somewhat unlikely and extreme example. A clerical student makes his first acquaintance with mental prayer in the seminary exercise of meditation. Customs vary in regard to this exercise, but in many seminaries meditation is made in common on a subject which was read publicly the previous evening. In the morning the 'points' are repeated at intervals during which the student is expected first to apply himself to the consideration of what he has heard, and then to produce suitable affections and resolutions. In the beginning it is probable that 'considerations' will predominate and that 'affections' or real prayer will play a comparatively minor part. And this is as it should be—in the beginning. As a sound foundation for a spiritual life, the student's knowledge of supernatural things must be developed, strong convictions must be formed, and consideration of divine truths is the natural means for these ends. But, little by little, his familiarity with the things of God grows; it grows through his attempts at prayer and through his studies. In prayer, therefore, considerations become less necessary, and should be replaced, to a very large extent, by 'acts' of various kinds. Now if such a student were to cling rigorously to the method of prayer by which he began; if, approaching his ordination and afterwards as a priest, he were to give as much time to considerations as in the beginning, he would be acting in a manner calculated to retard his advance in mental prayer. He would be like a grown or growing boy trying to walk with the tiny steps of a child. And just as a boy would find the effort to walk in such a manner irksome in the extreme, so it will be with a priest who continues to use a method of mental prayer no longer suited to his state.

This, of course, is an extreme case and is scarcely fully applicable to any priest. But it is possible that an individual priest might make this mistake in some degree. Of the normal path of progress in prayer and of the signs which indicate that one should leave a lower plane for a higher, we shall have more to say in later chapters.

Most priests, however, have a knowledge of the ways of prayer that makes this mistake unlikely, and will agree that this does not provide a solution for their own personal problems. Where, then, are we to look for the solution? To try to answer that question is our purpose in all that follows.

It is easy, too easy, to look upon our mental prayer as an isolated exercise, whose success depends on the regularity with which we perform it and the amount of effort we put into it. This, of course, is an error. Our whole priestly life is a unit; our love of God, of our neighbour, our growth in virtue and our progress in prayer are things which will always bear a proportion to each other. At the moment, however, we are concerned only with what is commonly described as the interior life of the priest and we shall concentrate on that. But even in this limited sphere, mental prayer does not stand apart by itself as something that can flourish independently; it is but one of those three fundamental elements of a healthy spiritual life, the other two being spiritual reading and reflection. What we mean in the present context by prayer is best summed up in the classic definition of St. Teresa: 'Mental

prayer, in my opinion, is nothing else than being on
terms of intimate friendship with God, frequently conversing in secret with him, who, we know, loves us.'
What we mean by reading and reflection we shall
strive to explain in the course of this chapter.

Meditation, as it is commonly understood, is a con-
densation of these three actions into one exercise. Our
suggestion is to divide them into at least two exercises.
One of these is to be, principally, spiritual reading;
the other is to be, principally, mental prayer as we have
described it. Reflection, the third element, can be
associated with either or both or may be done in an
informal way at some other hour of the day.

Within the limits of the present chapter, only a summary discussion of spiritual reading is possible; those
interested in a fuller treatment we would refer to what
we have written on the subject elsewhere.[1] It has two
main purposes; the first is to instruct us: the second is
to keep us in contact with the supernatural world, above
all in contact with the centre of that world, the Person
of our Saviour.

Spiritual reading is necessary for our instruction.
At first sight it might appear that a priest has little or
no need of such 'educative' spiritual reading. Every
priest has studied theology and scripture, and some, at
least, have acquired a profound knowledge of these
sacred matters. But it is well to remember that, even
in these subjects, there can be two distinct lines of approach, the purely speculative on the one hand, and on
the other an approach which seeks to apply the truths
learned to one's own life. Once again, for the sake of
clarity, let us take an extreme example. A student, let
us say, studies his theology solely with a view to pre-
eminence in examinations. If he has ability and diligence

he will succeed; when he finishes his studies he will have a good but purely speculative knowledge of theology. To put it in a popular phrase, he knows all the answers. But that knowledge could remain superficial in the sense that what he has learned has no effect on his outlook, his attitude, his life; he has more knowledge but he keeps it sealed off in the purely speculative department of his mind. It does not sink in and become part of himself, an active factor in his life. This case, where there is *no* point of contact between the sacred knowledge and the student's life, is, of course, next to impossible, but the hypothesis suggests a danger against which we priests must be on our guard. In our ministry, for instance, we must teach, preach and direct souls. For this we need knowledge, very considerable knowledge, which we can acquire only through reading and study. And there is always at least the possibility that the priest should make an unconscious distinction between his professional mind, so to speak, and his personal outlook.

To take another unlikely example, one could conceive the case of a man who studies ascetical and mystical theology in order to guide saintly souls, but who fails altogether to apply the principles he has learned to his own life. To put it in a word, the fact that a priest knows, speculatively, every proposition of theology is, in itself, no guarantee that his knowledge is of such a kind as will influence his life. That is why it may sometimes be necessary even for learned priests to take a 'refresher' course in theology and scripture with a view to applying the eternal truths to themselves.

But there is another and even more important reason for the necessity of spiritual reading. The world which we know by our senses and our intellect is ever palpably with us, proclaiming its presence with a thousand voices; the world of the supernatural we know only in the obscurity of Faith. As we have said elsewhere:[2] 'We read to keep the supernatural before our minds, to develop and maintain the sense of reality of the things we know by Faith, to keep our attention on the eternal life of our soul rather than our own interests and above all to keep alive within us the memory of the presence of our Lord so that we may live in touch and in union with him, talking to him, working with him, resting with him, always praying to him and in him.'

Pius X, in reminding priests that they are the friends of Christ, tells them in what their friendship must consist. 'To desire and to abhor the same things, that is the essence of friendship. Being friends of Christ, we are bound to have the mind of Christ.' 'To have the mind of Christ', to see all things through the eyes of Christ, that, in a word, is the second great purpose of spiritual reading. Spiritual reading alone will not, indeed, give us the mind of Christ; reflection and prayer must play their part, but as we see it, daily reading is the foundation for the other two exercises.

Regular spiritual reading is an excellent, even an essential, preparation for prayer. If our minds, through reading, are steeped in a knowledge of God, of Christ and of ourselves, if the whole world of the supernatural is a vivid reality to us, prayer becomes comparatively easy. St. Francis de Sales wrote that 'if prayer is the flame of the sanctuary lamp, reading is the oil which feeds it.' A priest who neglects spiritual reading and seeks to pray is trying to have flame without oil and cannot succeed. In some ways we regard daily spiritual reading as more important than prayer itself. Sometimes, of course, it cannot be done, but under ordinary circumstances a priest who neglects regular spiritual reading relinquishes all hope of progress in prayer.

Two questions may be asked in regard to spiritual reading : *what* are we to read and *how* are we to read. The answer to the first question depends upon so many variable factors that we can make little or no attempt to give a positive answer here. Individual needs and tastes must be taken into consideration. If a man, for instance, were fighting against discouragement, books which stress the difficulty of salvation or of perseverance would certainly be inadvisable, though they might be a healthy corrective for an individual takings things too casually. Tastes, too, should be considered; it does not serve any good purpose to read books which are completely uncongenial. To do so consistently might lead in time to a disgust for and even the abandonment of the exercise. Caution, however, is necessary in estimating the unsuitability of a book. There may be things which we are not always ready to have pointed out to us, and a consequent tendency to regard as unsuitable or uncongenial books which remind us of these things. We must be on our guard against self-deception and, as a precaution, the opinion of a competent friend who is willing and able to see things from our point of view is well worth having.

Pride of place, of course, must be given to the sacred scriptures, especially to the Gospels. There, above all, we meet and learn to know the historical Christ, and there is no need to emphasize how supremely important this is for every priest. We might give, in fact, a general principle for our guidance in spiritual reading: that we should concentrate especially on such books as are calculated to build up in our minds a living idea of Christ and our relations with him. If this purpose dominates the general tendency of our choice of books, they will be well chosen.

There are certain classics that should be read at one time or another. It would be pointless to turn this chapter into a bibliography and so we shall refer to only one of these—to the *Imitation*. It can tell us a lot about ourselves in an amazingly short time and men who read it for a few minutes daily will never regret the practice. Attention should be paid, too, to books which apply the truths of dogmatic theology to our spiritual lives. The theology of grace and the divine indwelling in particular is especially a section that should be read and re-read with a personal purpose in view. In fact we would regard this as the basis of all sound spirituality, and, for a most helpful summary of this doctrine, we cannot recommend too highly the book of Fr. de Jaegher S.J., *One With Jesus*.[3] Finally, in this matter of the application of dogma to our spiritual lives, the works of Dom Marmion are unexcelled.

Reading, of course, should be begun with a short prayer. We are going to listen to God and prayer is the proper approach to him. The practice of kneeling down for a moment is well worth while. We should read with care and attention; it will help us to form a right idea of how to read if we visualize a man examining the specifications of a new car or studying the details of an insurance policy. We shall discuss the question of reflection separately in a moment, but, as we have already said, it can easily be associated with spiritual reading—so, indeed, can prayer. During our reading, therefore, we should never be unwilling to pause and think when something strikes us, and, of course, any movement to pray by aspirations or silent looks at our Lord should always be given full play.

Mere reading, of course, is not enough; knowledge must be digested. This is the purpose of reflection, the second element in our interior life. It is very desirable that this reflection should be associated as closely as possible with our reading, but we should prefer to see it done quite informally and, if possible, quite spontaneously. Much, however, depends on individual temperament. Some men are reflective by nature and, if their reading interests them, they cannot help thinking it over in their spare moments. Much will depend too on a man's interest in divine things—an interest which itself will be the outcome of reading, reflection and prayer, for all these things are so closely connected and influence each other so intimately that it is only in theory that we can altogether separate them. Some priests, however, may find that the process of reflection is not, for them, at all spontaneous; these should apply themselves deliberately to the consideration of what they have read. This could be done while out for a walk, while smoking before a fire or in any other circumstances that lend themselves to thought. We find it hard to agree with the idea that reflection is something which *must* be done in the early morning, before breakfast, in the most uncomfortable circumstances. Perhaps we are biassed by our own total inability to think anything out at such a time. But we are so convinced of the need of reflection for a healthy spiritual life that we should prefer to see each priest choose for himself the time and place that is most congenial. The main thing is to think daily. When or where is of secondary importance. Reflection, or reflective reading, if carried out daily, takes the place of 'meditation.' We do not at all wish to do away with this exercise. Rather do we want to make it more elastic and more tolerable so that it can be suited to each man's circumstances and may come in time to dominate all his waking hours.

This thinking things out can easily develop into prayer. Some men think things out by talking them over with a friend. It should be possible for us, priests, to talk things over with him who has called us his friends. Our success in doing so will, indeed, depend on our habitual degree of intimacy with him, but we can at least do our best and very often we shall succeed in establishing with Christ a contact that is an excellent prayer. If we remember that it was by the companionship of Christ that the apostles were 'formed' spiritually, we shall realize how valuable is any exercise which puts us in touch with our Saviour. It does not seem that the apostles stood upon any ceremony with him. St. Peter even rebuked him. It is true, of course, that we are not in the same position as the apostles. To them Christ was physically and sensibly present, while we can make contact with him only through Faith. Our point of view is also quite different, for, unlike the apostles, we know the whole of the story which they were only gradually learning. But we have need of him no less than they and anything that brings us into his company is well worth while. Indeed our very need of him is our reason for being certain that he is seeking us. Did he not tell us that he is the Good Shepherd, come to seek that which was lost?

Our attempts, then, to turn our reflections into a discussion with Christ can be the beginning of a life of close union with him. And it is not at all necessary that we should always be talking to him of high and holy things. He who created everything is surely interested in all that he has made and we may therefore comment to him on all that comes under our observation. The conversation of two friends may be of quite trivial things, yet it serves as an expression of friendship and helps to develop it. Our Lord himself insisted that we are his friends. We can surely pay him the compliment of taking him at his word.

The development, however, of this type of informal conversation with our Divine Lord depends greatly on the sincerity of our friendship. If we insist on following our own will in opposition to his, we cannot feel at our ease with him. But there is something else which can interfere with the comradeship of which we have been speaking. We may have formed a wrong picture of him or we may have an exaggerated notion of what he expects from us. We must be careful to see that such is not the case. He is our Saviour, not yet our Judge; he 'receiveth sinners', and is not surprised to find that we are not saints. He never expects us to do more than is prudent, nor does he demand that we should attack all our imperfections at once. This is why a sound grasp of the principles of the spiritual life is so important for us. There are enough real obstacles to the divine union without our adding imaginary ones, of our own making, to the list. Anything savouring of Jansenism or rigorism would be disastrous. If, for example, a priest imagines that a life of intimacy with Christ precludes all human pleasures, he will not persevere long in such intimacy. Our Lord does not break bruised reeds or extinguish smoking flax.

Our discussion on reflection has brought us far afield, has brought us, in fact, into the realm of mental prayer itself. This is not surprising, for just as reading gives rise to reflection, so reflection merges almost naturally into prayer. The relations of these three elements of our interior life, one to another, are many, subtle and delicate; reading and reflection will have their effect on our prayer and prayer, in its turn, will have a profound influence on the spirit in which we read and reflect. But the fundamental connection between them can, perhaps, be best made clear by a metaphor. If reading is regarded as a root, then reflection is the stalk which springs up from the root; prayer is the flower which, while depending on root and stalk, is the crowning and the glory of both. And so, if priests sometimes find mental prayer almost impossible, we think that, instead of longing vainly for the petals of prayer which fail to appear, they should concentrate rather on the root and the stalk. If we take care of reading and reflection, mental prayer will, broadly speaking, take care of itself. But the great test is the test of practice, and if priests do as we suggest, we have little doubt that they will soon experience the truth of what we say for themselves.

Of mental prayer itself we shall speak in our next chapter.

[1] Cf. *This Tremendous Lover* (Mercier Press) and *Difficulties in Mental Prayer* (Gill)

[2] *This Tremendous Lover*

[3] Burns, Oates & Washbourne

CHAPTER THREE

STARTING TO PRAY

IN the previous chapters we have suggested that three things are fundamental for the interior life, namely: spiritual reading, reflection and private prayer. These three must find their place in each day's programme. As a rule, it will be sufficient to set aside a time for reading and a time for prayer. Reflection, in many cases, will spring spontaneously from these two exercises; if not, then, of course, some provision should be made for it, but it need not be done formally; in fact it is often better to make our reflections while walking or sitting down or, say, working in the garden. Some men find they think better in noisy surroundings, on the top of a tram, or in a busy street, but, as a rule, a certain degree of quiet is helpful. In our last chapter we tried to discuss reading and reflection, but found that we were continually recurring to prayer. The three are inseparably connected and cannot be adequately treated apart. In this chapter we propose to pay closer attention to the exercise of prayer.

One important point about prayer—we are now speaking of what is usually called mental prayer—is that it is not just one more exercise added to a number of others in the spiritual life. It is a summing-up of all those exercises. It is an expression of our attitude to

God, and it depends very closely upon how that attitude affects the rest of our life. We cannot pray sincerely unless our attitude to God is sincere. And our attitude to God is *not* sincere, if we deliberately prevent it from affecting our actions, especially when such prevention is habitual. That is why, to our mind, discussion of the 'technique' of prayer is more theoretical than practical unless one takes into consideration as well the whole of our spiritual life. That is why, in discussing our daily short period of prayer, we shall frequently have to digress to discuss many other aspects of our lives. For the real difficulty of praying has its roots outside prayer. If the 'remote' preparation for prayer is sound, little else is required to succeed in prayer; but that remote preparation is very far-reaching; it includes everything that we do. Yet, on the other hand, the way we do everything else depends on our prayer, so that while prayer in practice is quite simple, its discussion may be very involved.

The usual prescription for the beginning of mental prayer is to put ourselves in the presence of God. One might, perhaps, prefer to express it differently, but the idea is excellent. If we are going to speak to God, we must get in touch with him. That, however, is not so much a question of putting ourselves in his presence as of making him present to us by adverting to his presence, for in many ways he is always with us. Different men will do that in different ways. When prayer is made in the church the Real Presence in the Blessed Sacrament is often the focus of our attention. Despite the excellence of such a practice there are many great advantages to be gained by attending rather to the divine presence in our own souls, where that is found helpful. If there is difficulty in doing this, one way of overcoming it is to make a spiritual communion—a word or two will suffice—and then to proceed as if one has just received our Lord sacramentally.

But the point we regard as capital in all this is that early on in prayer we must make sure to catch God's eye, to look him in the face, as it were, even though it be only for a moment. To realize the importance of this one has only to imagine the meeting of two friends between whom there has been a tiny estrangement. They can talk fluently and freely for a long time about indifferent things and still part without any change in their strained relations as long as they do not look each other in the face. But the normal man cannot look his friend in the face and maintain his estrangement. He must either make it up or break it up. So it is when we go to pray. We can 'pray' at great length with a wealth of words and still retain a determination to say 'no' to God on some point, as long as we do not 'catch his eye.' But if we stop talking and fooling ourselves with our own words, and just for one tiny second look our Lord in the face, then—like St. Peter—we cannot continue in our cowardice and coldness, we must give him what he wants.

If we achieved nothing else in half an hour's prayer than that one look into the face of Jesus, our time would be well spent and its fruit immeasurable. Such an experience, if it comes to us every day, will produce a great effect on our spiritual life and have a considerable influence on our prayer. Henceforth our prayer must be sincere; we realize that we must mean what we say. Fine words and fine ideas have nothing to do with our prayer. It is not like composing a speech or writing an essay. It is a question of being honest with God and with oneself. Accordingly, our flow of words dries up and we stammer; we start to say something and then, realizing our own insincerity, we stop again. This is an excellent development in prayer, and these stammered words and phrases are far more valuable than the most eloquent and illuminated colloquies which, by the way, are very often more like soliloquies. 'Affections', of course, are what we are aiming at. But a sincere doubt about the sincerity of our hesitant 'My God, I love thee!' is often more in accordance with truth than a long protestation of undying love.

We need never be afraid to draw our Lord's attention to the lack of complete sincerity in our protestations. This is a point where many people make a mistake. For a time they can 'pray', that is, they can keep on talking to God. Then they begin to question the sincerity of their statements and they come to realize how little real truth is in them. Sometimes they become discouraged and give up prayer as something outside their scope; they feel they are not sincere enough to talk to God.

That brings us to a point that we consider to be of the utmost importance in prayer as well as in the whole spiritual life. We must have the correct notion of God's attitude to us. Now, the first Person of the Blessed Trinity is our Father, and the authentic portrait of his attitude to us is painted for us by the lips of Infinite Truth in the parable of the prodigal son. And the third Person of the Blessed Trinity is our Sanctifier, whom the liturgy calls 'the remission of our sins', so that we do not need to be saints to go to him; he knows that we are sinners and that our sanctification must come from him. So, then, even though we know ourselves to be sinners, we have no real reason to be afraid to approach the Father or the Holy Ghost.

But it is through the second Person that we are to go to God and his attitude to us is of the greatest importance. And his attitude is perfectly expressed by his name, for he is called Jesus ' because he shall save his people from their sins.' He is, then, our *Saviour*. This we must never forget. We must make it the foundation of all our relations with him. He is always ready to save us from our sins and from our shortcomings. Thus, those very failings which tend to inhibit our prayer can be made the reason for a very close bond between us. They need not separate us from him or drive us away. 'This man receiveth sinners', and we need not be afraid to approach him. In fact, like St. Paul, we should glory in our infirmities that the power of Christ may dwell in us. Our very defects may lead to a very close union with our Saviour. We must be quite clear and definite about this point. Divine union is not something reserved for spotless or angelic souls. It is the essential foundation of even the lowest degree of true Christian living, for a man cannot be in the state of grace unless he is so closely united to God as to share in the divine nature! Our Lord himself has made it quite clear that he wants to be intimate with us. If the institution of the Blessed Eucharist be not proof enough, let us remember the text: 'Behold, I stand at the gate, and knock. If any man shall hear my voice, and open to me the door, I will come in to him, and will sup with him, and he with me.'[1]

We need not, then, be afraid to be intimate with our Lord in our private prayers. The very fact that we are sinners and need his saving power is sufficient justification for our drawing close to him, and it is our reason for asking for close union with him so that his power may *dwell* in us.

There is only one type of sinner who cannot be at his ease with God, and that is the man who intends to continue sinning. To glory in *that* infirmity, and to hope that the power of Christ will dwell in a soul deliberately defiant of the will of Christ, is worse than presumption. The case, however, is quite different if a man *wants* to give up sin, and yet experiences difficulty in doing so. Such a man need have no fear of appealing to our Lord's saving grace. For it is precisely such a man that our Lord wants to save.

These considerations will suggest that one of the best starting-points for private prayer is a gentle act of sorrow for sin and a desire not to sin again. Starting from that, we can develop with our omnipotent Saviour a colloquy which will be a perfect prayer. This, however, is but one example. One can start from any other act— adoration or faith, for example—and let the conversation flow from that starting-point. The thing we wish to emphasize here is that prayer is a conversation (it may be a silent one) with Jesus, and we must be careful that we regard him in the correct light lest a wrong outlook should stifle our part in it. To our mind, the fact that it is to our Lord that we are talking is far more important than what we say to him. Talking to Christ develops our friendship and intimacy with him and that is what is so desirable.

If we recall the trivialities which serve as topics for conversation between friends or lovers and remember that the persons concerned are interested not so much in these trivialities as in each other, we may be encouraged to allow ourselves a little more liberty in our choice of subject matter for conversation with him who called us his friends. The fact that we have made provision elsewhere in reading and reflection for the harvest that is usually expected from meditation may also ease our mind on this point. The important thing in prayer is not so much the choosing of the subject as keeping in touch with our Lord. And for that reason we need not worry too much about the subject of our prayer as long as we can talk to God about it. Even distractions, therefore, can be made a starting-point for a colloquy with him. But what is of importance is to make sure that it is really to our Lord that we are talking and not just to ourselves or to some unfounded fantasy of our imagination. That is why it is so necessary to pause now and then to catch God's eye. Even in mental prayer we are liable to harden our hearts and go on praying so that we may not hear his voice!

We have commenced our discussion of mental prayer by considering it as a conversation with God for two reasons. The first is that we have already provided for the other aspects of it by insistence on reading and reflection; the second, that the conversational aspect is not always given its proper place. Until one has reached some degree of simplified prayer, conversation with God is the really important part of prayer both as an aim and as a practice. The rest, to some extent at any rate, is rather an introduction to prayer, a means to an end. But because the end is often unattainable—because there are so many occasions when we can find nothing to say—then one must have recourse to the means, one must meditate.

Before, however, discussing the use of such means, let us note another way of sustaining prayerful contact with God. We can make use of some favourite formula of vocal prayer, reciting it slowly and deliberately with plenty of pauses, and making the words our own by dwelling on them. A gentle effort to mean each word and to utter it sincerely will often produce the desired result. The Psalms afford excellent material for this way of praying; but one should not linger over obscure or difficult texts, but be content with those verses that say something which we want to say. Any formula of prayer drawn from our memory or from a book can be used in this way. One book which many will find helpful is *The Sufferings of Our Lord Jesus Christ* by Fr. Thomas of Jesus O.S.A. It is a translation of an old Portuguese work in which every second chapter is a prayer personally addressed to our Lord. Each one, however, will have his own favourite, and old friends are the best friends; we do not want a book which is so new to us that we are continually tempted to go on to see what comes next.

Even books which are not prayer-books can be used to feed the flames—or perhaps we should say, kindle the spark—of prayer. Some people find that they can get on best by using a suitable spiritual book. They read it sentence by sentence and pause in between to make acts inspired by what they have just read. In such a case, care must always be taken that the exercise of prayer does not become mere spiritual reading.

The book used must, therefore, be carefully chosen. It should be one which makes the reader pause and think rather than one which tends to carry him on further. Here, too, old friends are the best.

Reflection—however it may arise—can often be turned into prayer; instead of talking to ourselves in our thoughts, we can talk over the matter with our Lord. This is a possibility which should be borne in mind when there is question of approaching prayer by the conventional way of methodical meditation. Of methodical meditation it is hardly necessary to treat here at any length. There are many excellent books on the subject; those written by Fr. Egan S.J. and by Fr. Kearney C.S.Sp. will be of great help. (The chapter on 'The Prayer of Stupidity' in Fr. Egan's book, *The House of Peace*, is invaluable and should be familiar to every one who wants to pray). All we wish to say here on the subject is that any priest who adds to his theological studies the daily practice of spiritual reading and reflection may allow himself considerable latitude in following the more rigid and detailed prescriptions laid down by some writers. He should never forget that in regard to prayer the preludes and considerations are means to an end; once the end, namely praying, has been attained, the means may be set aside for the moment.

However, a priest should not carry this emancipation so far as to free himself from having some subject of prayer ready at hand upon which he may fall back if all else fails. This may be the subject of earlier spiritual reading; it may be some point in the liturgy of the day; it may be one of the mysteries of the Rosary or one of the Stations of the Cross. These latter have the advantage of being arranged in a familiar order so that they are ready to hand. If care is not taken to provide a prepared subject, prayer may become a mere series of distractions or an idle reverie. We cannot, however, exhaust the subject of prayer in this chapter, and as we should prefer to link up further discussion with the possibility of advance in prayer, we shall postpone it to later on. Let us here advert to another point which also calls for further treatment but is mentioned here as it may help those who are looking for the cause of difficulty in praying.

Success at prayer is not—primarily, at least— a

matter of technique or of method. Admittedly technique and methods have something to do with it, but their role is quite secondary. What is of primary importance is the fervour of one's life and the degree of one's willingness to follow the example of our Lord. For us priests it can all be summed up in one question: how sincerely do we say our Mass? That, perhaps, is rather summary; but the life of a priest should be an unfolding of what he promises when he says Mass. There are, of course, other springs of devotion, so that a man's fervour may outrun his appreciation of the Mass, but in the long run it is the Mass that matters. For in the Mass a priest acts in the name of Christ. He is so closely associated with the priesthood of Christ that he speaks in the first person when he consecrates. He offers Christ's sacrifice. But in Christ's sacrifice, Christ is victim as well as priest; he offers himself. Do we imitate him? Do we realize that he also offers us? Do we consent to that? Because if we do not, there can hardly be any close and deep friendship between us and our prayer will be rather a conventional greeting between business partners, so to speak, than a heart-to-heart talk between friends. Where there is a deliberate intention to continue wounding him by a habit of sin, friendship and prayer are extremely difficult. Even a deliberate refusal to co-operate with the inspirations of his grace, asking us for some sacrifice to which we are not bound, will be a great obstacle to our success at prayer. But even where there is no clear-cut purpose contrary to his will, there are still attitudes of mind which hinder prayer. We may, for example, be afraid that generosity in his service is going to impose intolerable burdens upon us. We forget that he has assured us that his yoke is easy and his burden light, and we priests should know him well enough by now to know that he does not break the bruised reed.

An unconscious fear of some unwelcome demand from him is very often at the root of our problems in prayer. We either keep on talking empty words or filling our imagination with empty pictures so as to leave him no chance of speaking in our souls, or else we erect some sort of a barrier between us so that we cannot look each other in the face. That is why one cannot discuss prayer without discussing the whole spiritual life. Until a man wants—at least to some extent—to give himself to our Lord, prayer will always be penance rather than a pleasure, an embarrassment rather than an embrace. After all, he himself warned us that we cannot be his disciples unless we are willing to deny ourselves, to take up our cross daily and to follow him. Unless we are willing to do that, we cannot be his sincere friends. But prayer is the heart-to-heart conversation of a friend of God with his Divine Lover, so that without such friendship and all it entails, prayer will always be difficult.

[1] Apoc. III, 20

CHAPTER FOUR

THE PRIEST AND THE MASS

At the close of our last chapter we dwelt on the connection between mental prayer and the general tone of a priest's spiritual life. To one with any experience of the spiritual life, this connection soon becomes quite obvious. Without mental prayer in some form or other the spiritual life will not flourish; but, on the other hand, unless the spiritual life is healthy, mental prayer soon becomes difficult. It becomes clear, then, that mental prayer is not merely one particular exercise of the spiritual life, tucked away in its own corner of the day, for it is, in fact, both a source and a summary of our relations with God. If we are not sincere in our service of God, we cannot be sincere in our prayer, we cannot talk to him or even meet him without constraint and uneasiness. In actual fact the whole spiritual life is a unity; all our actions should, in a wide sense of the word, be a prayer, an expression of our devotion to God. Consider but one example given by our Lord's life. Entering into the world he said to the Father: 'Behold I come to do thy will.' And we know that he never ceased to do that will and to fulfil that prayer of consecration, for he was obedient unto death, even to the death of the Cross. In fact, the very sacrifice of Calvary which ended our Lord's life in the eyes of the Jews was but a summing-up and a perfect expression of the whole of his life.

Now, we priests offer that very same sacrifice every time we say Mass. If we want to follow him, if we want to live a spiritual life, we must endeavour to *mean* the Mass, to be sincere in what we say when we offer sacrifice to God. And we must also endeavour to see that our day's work and actions are in harmony with our daily sacrifice. It is true that the theology of the Mass is very deep and complicated. The immensity of the sacrifice of Christ, as High Priest, of himself as Victim is so overwhelming that we are apt to overlook our personal association with him as Priest *and as Victim*. It is this latter association that is especially relevant here. In the encyclical on the Mystical Body of Christ we are reminded that not only does Christ offer himself in the Mass by the ministry of the priests, but that he also offers each of his members. So that when we priests are offering Mass, we cannot avoid offering ourselves. Unfortunately, we tend to overlook that fact. We feel, perhaps, in some vague way that although sacrifice in the Old Law was an external sign of an interior sacrifice, the offerer offering the victim as evidence of his will to offer himself to God, yet since Christ has replaced the sacrifice of the Old by his unique sacrifice of the New Law, there is no need to worry about our personal part in the matter. Even if this were true—even if sacrifice had lost its function as a visible sign of our invisible sacrifice— yet, since Christ offers us in the Mass, we must be prepared to take our place with him as victims. We are his friends, not merely his servants. And the mark of friendship in this connection is, as Pius X pointed out to us priests, summed up in the phrase: *idem velle*, *idem nolle*, to have the mind of Christ, to share his views, to share his devotion to the Father.

We cannot too earnestly urge the importance, for every priest, of this personal participation in the sacrifice of Christ. The point is so important that we feel justified in citing some authorities. St. Thomas, speaking of the priest's Communion at Mass, writes: 'Whoever offers a sacrifice ought to become a partaker in it, because the external sacrifice which is offered is a sign of the interior sacrifice by which one offers oneself to God. Hence by the fact that he partakes in the sacrifice (namely by Communion) the offerer shows that he really shares in the interior sacrifice.'[1] Pius XI was most insistent on the need for such participation even by the laity. One text from *Miserentissimus Deus*, the encyclical on reparation, will suffice. 'We must, then, form together in the august sacrifice of the Blessed Eucharist the act of immolation made by the priest with that of the faithful so that they too may offer themselves up as a "living sacrifice, holy and pleasing unto God." Therefore St. Cyprian dared to affirm that "the sacrifice of our Lord is not complete as far as our sanctification is concerned unless our offerings and sacrifices correspond to his Passion".' The late Holy Father Pius XII developed the point in his encyclical, *Mediator Dei*. He desires 'that all the faithful should be aware that *to participate in the Eucharistic sacrifice is their chief duty and supreme dignity*.' He continues by quoting St. Paul: 'Let this mind be in you which was also in Christ Jesus', and exhorts the faithful: 'Together with him and through him let them make their oblation and in union with him let them offer up themselves.' Explaining the above text of St. Paul, the Holy Father warns us that it 'requires that all Christians should

possess, as far as is humanly possible, the same dispositions as those which the Divine Redeemer had
when he offered himself in sacrifice: that is to say, they
should, in a humble attitude of mind, pay adoration,
honour, praise and thanksgiving to the supreme majesty
of God. Moreover, it means that they must assume to
some extent the character of a victim, that they deny
themselves as the Gospel commands, that freely and of
their own accord they do penance and that each de-
tests and satisfies for his sins. It means, in a word, that
we must all undergo with Christ a mystical death on the
Cross, so that we can apply to ourselves the words of
St. Paul: "With Christ I am nailed to the Cross".'

This exhortation is addressed to the laity. If this is
their 'chief duty and supreme privilege', how much
more is it ours? If these are the dispositions appropriate
for those who assist at Mass, what must be expected of
us priests who such a special part fulfil in offering
it? At least, we too must apply to ourselves the
words of St. Paul: 'With Christ, I am nailed to the Cross.'

Lest, however, a wrong emphasis on the necessity of
sacrifice should make our vocation appear too negative
or too gloomy, let us recall St. Augustine's description
of true sacrifice: 'Omne opus quod agitur ut sancta
societate inhaereamus Deo', and be assured that the
ultimate purpose of sacrifice is not so much the des-
struction of ourselves as the uniting of ourselves to God.
Many priests will get a new light on the Mass from the
translation of Canon Masure's book, *The Christian
Sacrifice*. But whatever we do, we should leave nothing
undone to come to some proper appreciation of what
we are about when we offer Mass. A proper view and a
sincere celebration can and must be the centre and
source of a most holy spiritual life.

But our devotion and our dispositions must not be confined merely to the time of Mass. If we offer ourselves as victims, we do not cease to be victims when we leave the altar. We must be prepared to have God take us at our word. We have given ourselves to him in the same way as Jesus Christ gave himself to his Father; we cannot but expect that the Father will treat us as he treated his Son. In fact, it is for that very purpose that Jesus has called us to be his priests—that by sharing in his life and death, we may share in his joy and his glory. Patience, then, has a very special significance for us priests; patience, especially in the ordinary trials of the ordinary day's routine, makes us participators in the Passion of Christ. And indeed every priest would do well to take patience as the subject of his particular examen for, say, a month every year. Our own spiritual lives would benefit from it and so too would those with whom we have to work.

We must strive, then, to practise patience as a means of carrying out our offering of ourselves in our daily Mass. But there is another point to which we must give particular attention, a weakness which we must be careful to avoid. If we have truly given ourselves to God, self-seeking must no longer be a principle of our actions. Fr. Grou S.J., in his wonderful book, *Manual for Interior Souls*, puts before us an ideal which may seem too high but which contains the secret of peace and holiness. He writes: 'The first result of our devotion to God (and, we may add, of our sacrifice of ourselves in the Mass) should be the union of our hearts with the adoration and annihilation of Jesus in his Mother's womb. *When we give ourselves to God, it is unfortunately too often with a view to becoming something great, something distinguished, pride and self-love exercising a strong influence over our dedication to God.* Let us now give ourselves to him with no other view than to be entirely consumed and destroyed, with no other desire than to sacrifice for ever all self-esteem, all anxiety for our spiritual exaltation, all personal interests, all views, all considerations and reflections concerned with self. Let us once and for all lose sight of ourselves and give up our being to God alone.'

Some readers may feel that such an ideal is too high for a diocesan priest. And indeed one cannot help sympathizing with such an objection, for Fr. Grou is asking for a very complete sacrifice of oneself. Yet the matter may appear in a different light if we recall the words of the bishop who ordained us: 'Understand what you do, imitate what you handle.' We 'handle' the sacrifice of Christ, we are asked to imitate it. Such a high ideal will, perhaps, become more acceptable to us if we read the encyclical on the liturgy, *Mediator Dei*, of our late Holy Father, Pius XII. He is writing for all the faithful but time and time again he returns to the need of their making an offering of themselves in union with the Christian sacrifice. To *them* he writes: 'In order that the oblation by which the faithful offer the Divine Victim in this sacrifice to the Heavenly Father may have its full effect, it is necessary that the people add something else, namely the offering of themselves as a victim.' If that is what the Holy Father required from the laity, what did he ask from *us*, his priests? Truly can we exhort each other: 'Let that mind be in you which was also in Christ Jesus!' And it is no impracticable ideal, for we have the power of Christ at our disposal. By him and in him we have all fullness so that nothing is wanting to us in any grace.

[1] *Summa Theol.* III, 83-4

CHAPTER FIVE

LIFE OF PRAYER

IT would be a great mistake for any priest to think that the necessity for daily mental prayer arises merely from Canon Law or Church discipline, for its importance is intrinsic and is based on its essential connection with the spiritual life. But it would also be a mistake to regard it as an exercise at which success depends on talents or application and can be measured, so to speak, as we measure success in a sermon or some purely intellectual exercise. For nowhere else in the spiritual life can apparent failure so easily conceal real achievement. Let us review the position for a moment. The normal approach to prayer is by reading and reflection. Many writers include these in prayer itself and indeed some seem to make the whole exercise consist in remembering and reflecting with a few minor acts added by way of an accidental winding-up of the whole. To emphasize the importance of the *prayer* element, we have in these chapters suggested that reading and reflection be made separate exercises and that they be used at the time given to mental prayer only in so far as they are necessary as a means to achieve prayer. Since, however, prayer, as we have just admitted, is very often achieved in apparent failure instead of by perceptible success, many will wonder whether there is anything left after reading and reflection have been relinquished, and will decide that, since in their case prayer seems so difficult to achieve, they had better occupy themselves with reflection or even with reading if reflection does not succeed.

This is a point on which we cannot compromise. It is quite true that there can be no spiritual life without reading and reflection. In some equivalent form or other they are absolutely essential and it is by neglect of them that so many of us allow our spiritual lives to decline. A healthy spiritual life must be nourished; but it must also be exercised, and prayer is one of its most important exercises. Intellect and will have both their part to play in the spiritual life. At prayer it is mainly the will which is to be exercised. For prayer is not merely an intellectual activity. It is a reaching-out of the soul to God, not merely to know him but still more to love him and to be united to him. It is true that there is much prayer in the daily life of the priest. He frequently, so to speak, meets God and acts in his name in the course of his liturgical and apostolic activities. But most of this is done in an official capacity. It is quite possible for a man, speaking officially, to condemn roundly and resolutely things which in his private life he condones. And there are many other official activities which can be performed in an impersonal way despite an external appearance of zeal and emotion. In fact, one of the dangers to which a priest is exposed is that of thinking that by denouncing vice and demanding virtue he has thereby fulfilled all justice. This possibility of divorce between one's official and one's private life is also found in the matter of prayer, and that is why no priest can be satisfied with the official prayers of his daily duties unless he is also personally and whole-heartedly involved in them. And if his own personal feelings are involved in his public prayers, he will long for the opportunity of pouring them out in private. So that, in any event, private prayer becomes of capital importance. For most of us unfortunately it becomes of importance, not because we feel a need of relieving a pent-up torrent of devotion and desire, but because of our lack of such ardent supernatural aspirations.

The seed for the growth of such aspirations is sown by reading and cultivated by reflection but can be brought to life only in prayer—in private, personal prayer. In such a prayer a priest must go to meet God; thinking about him is not enough. This meeting with God is not a matter of eloquence or originality, of depth of thought or extent of learning but of divine grace and human correspondence. We cannot go to God unless he, in his fatherliness, draws us. And we can go no further towards him than his grace enables us to do. What we can do is to ask for his grace and to dispose ourselves for it; to count upon sufficient grace to enable us to do that can hardly be presumptuous. So that the first step of our ascent to God in prayer must be to ask sincerely and humbly, in willing acknowledgement and acceptance of our helplessness, for grace to seek God and to go to him.

The second step is to dispose ourselves for the reception of such grace and to prepare to co-operate with it. Since our will plays such an important part in this going to God, the detaching of our will from any deliberate quest opposed to our purpose is a most important preparation for prayer. That, perhaps, is where many of us fail. Our wills have attached themselves to something opposed to our quest of God, something he has forbidden, something he has asked us to sacrifice, something which we are afraid of being asked to renounce. We do not want God earnestly enough to leave our nets and our nothings—for is not the whole world and our own selves nothing without God?—to go in search of him. Some, perhaps, may be discouraged by this conclusion, but unnecessarily. Since it is only by God's grace that we can detach ourselves so thoroughly from all else, we need never be afraid to admit to God our defects and our shortcomings. We need never be afraid to tell him that even though the spirit is willing, the flesh is weak. We need not even fear to remind him that our spirit is far from being what it should be. He is our Father. He is our Saviour. He is our Sanctifier. It is he who is to pour love into our hearts and to compel our rebellious wills to come to his wedding feast. And very often he withholds his assistance until we learn our own helplessness in aridity and 'failure' at prayer. Yet such aridity, such failure, is a very great advantage. For in the spiritual life there is no one so weak as the man who does not suspect his own weakness. The only men who are at all truly sure of their power to go to God are those who are quite convinced that all their sufficiency is from God; that the only strength they have is God's strength and grace.

For that reason a helpless, drowsy, distracted, sterile, dreary ten minutes spent at mental prayer is—in so far as it is a perfect expression of our own position with regard to God—a very good prayer. It expresses the truth far better than the most eloquent phrases or the most ardent feelings. It leaves us nothing of which to be proud but it offers God much to excite his compassion. And it is only when God has compassion on us that we can succeed in finding him in prayer! By

way of consolation the writer might add that, as far as
he can see, such 'unsuccessful' prayer is the normal experience of souls who are truly spiritual after the initial
stages of sensible fervour and devotional discovery
have been passed.

Perhaps the following quotation from such an
authority as Fr. M. Egan S.J. will help. In his excellent
book, *The House of Peace*,[1] he has a chapter entitled
'The Prayer of Stupidity', which commences: 'Mgr.
Ronald Knox, in one of two admirable articles on
prayer which he contributed to the *Clergy Review* (June
and July 1939), recommends what he quaintly calls the
Prayer of Stupidity, as a kind of prayer suitable to
souls of ordinary calibre who are in search of God.
It consists in a sort of general awareness of God, with
a vague and more or less indiscriminate movement of
the will towards him. The soul is in what we may call
a prayerful attitude, which may or may not receive a
specific direction or determination through particular
acts of the mind or will. It is a kind of prayer that is
familiar to many who, perhaps, have not recognized it
as prayer at all; they have thought of it either as a
failure to pray, for which they feel more or less blameworthy, or at best an inoffensive way of putting in the
time allotted to prayer by rule or custom. Nevertheless
it is really prayer. It may be very imperfect, full of
distractions, many of them ascribable to sloth or
negligence, barely worthy of the name of prayer; but
on the other hand it may, without losing its vagueness
and amorphous character, be very pleasing to God and
very sanctifying to the soul.' Fr. Egan then goes on to
consider the progress in prayer of a Jesuit novice trained
in discursive prayer. 'It is, I think', he writes, 'the experience of many Jesuits, perhaps of most, that the

power of meditating, of acquiring and turning over spiritual ideas and using them to enkindle their wills, grew and increased in them for some time, but did not continue to grow. On the contrary, after a longer or shorter period, these spiritual ideas, "lights" about our Lord's life, or about eternal truths, came less and less easily in the time of prayer. They might come at other times . . . . But at times of prayer when one was alone with God, the mind seemed to relapse into dullness, into an uncouth and stupid silence broken by a few half-formed acts and by a multitude of distractions.'

There are two points in the above quotation which we wish to underline. The first is that this 'failure' at prayer is really an advance in prayer. The second is the nature of this prayer so well summed up in the last phrase: 'an uncouth and stupid silence, broken by a few half-formed acts and by a multitude of distractions.' A little thought will show us that if prayer is a meeting with God, the very finding of God in prayer might be expected to produce just such an attitude on our part. As long as the person to whom we are praying is vividly portrayed in our imagination, in our own terms, so to speak, it is not surprising that we should be able to talk freely and earnestly. But when all creatures of our own imagination are removed and when God really begins to manifest himself to our souls, what adequate speech is left for us? Is not silence his fitting praise? Indeed, one often suspects that much o the fervour and facility which some souls experience at prayer is the result of finding themselves rather than of finding God. Such facile fervour decreases as one progresses along the road which St. John the Baptist summarized as decrease of self and increase of Christ.

On the other hand one must not overlook Fr. Egan's

suggestion that in some cases such a performance at prayer may be due to our own sloth and negligence. To go to God we have to leave our nets. If we do not dispose ourselves at the beginning of our prayer and put aside all distracting preoccupations with creatures, we need not be surprised at the result. The remedy lies in our own hands. But the remedy is not to return to meditation; it is to turn to God with our whole heart. Obviously this whole-hearted turning to God greatly depends on the general tenor of our spiritual lives. Our prayer will often reflect the shortcomings of our other activities. If we deliberately prefer creatures to God, such a preference will certainly fetter our will when we try to pursue God at prayer. Nevertheless it is by praying, by asking, by knocking and by seeking that we shall obtain the grace and the strength to break our fetters and to seek God with all our heart.

If then a priest finds that his prayer is a failure, let him not give in to the temptation to abandon prayer. Provided there is not an obvious cause on his part, provided that he daily reads and reflects, he need have no scruple about continuing what seems such a futile activity. It is only when one decides to omit prayer because of such 'failure' that one learns by sad experience how valuable it was and how great an effect it had, for all its apparent futility, in sanctifying us. It is practically impossible to persevere in sincere attempts at daily prayer, even though the attempt seems to fail, while persevering in any deliberate infidelity to God. But if one gives up the attempt at prayer infidelities flourish unchecked. The proper prescription for a soul whose prayer is 'stupid' is patience and abandonment. We must be content to be beggars before God, to realize that our spiritual poverty is our most valuable

title to God's bounty; and we must embrace such
poverty, gladly relying on the merciful compassion of
God, who himself is our Father, our Saviour and our
Sufficiency.

[4] Gill

CHAPTER SIX

DIFFICULTIES IN PRAYER

To avoid misunderstanding, let us here summarize our view about the practice of meditation and prayer for priests. We have insisted on the necessity for daily reading, daily reflection and daily prayer. As a support or scaffolding for these, we ask each priest to set apart a period in his daily timetable for spiritual reading, and also one for private prayer. The reading is to be done reflectively; it may be interspersed with short periods of silent reflection or of aspiratory prayer. We hope that this will lead a priest to reflect informally during the freer periods of the day, and we would suggest a periodic checking-up to see that this is being done. Meditation, in this sense of reflection fed by reading, can never be deliberately dispensed with. It is to this exercise we look for the formation and maintenance of convictions, for their application to our daily life—though this will call for some special examination of conscience—and for the making real of those darkly-seen truths of faith which are the mainspring of the spiritual life.

Many writers condense all these things into one exercise of 'meditation' or 'mental prayer'. Our fear is that by doing this the need for prayer in the real sense of the word may be overlooked and receive too little attention. For that reason we make prayer a separate exercise. We freely admit that, for many, such a special period for prayer may have to be approached immediately through reading and reflection, but we insist that these should be used only in so far as they are necessary as a means to an end, and that in this special exercise of prayer they should be given no other function than to put us in touch with God and to start us praying to him.

Supposing then that all this has been done regularly, and that there has been made a reasonable and sustained effort to live a spiritual life in accordance with the convictions acquired in reading and reflection and with the promises made in prayer, what is going to happen at prayer? Normally one may expect to find prayer becoming more and more affective; one speaks with an increasing facility to God; 'acts' come with a fair fluency and our prayer, by analogy, resembles the conversation of two good friends. This at least should be the expectation of every priest, because Christ does not call him his servant but his friend. This friendship however is not a static thing. It should develop. On our side there will be an advance in the knowledge and understanding of our Friend's mind and ways; in this sense mutual understanding and sympathy will grow. This progress will certainly affect our conversation with him. Our words become charged with a new meaning; in fact, single words begin to replace sentences. When we do achieve sentences, they have a manifold significance. Our whole utterance simplifies itself. We converse with only a few words or even with none at all. A glance, a smile, even a silence, can say all that we want to say to one who knows us so well. We may even lose the desire to say anything; all we want to do is to remain quietly in his company. Such a change in our prayer need not surprise us. It is similar to the development of human friendship. Grace of course is at work, but grace here seems to adapt itself to the ordinary ways of human nature. Of course, this type of prayer depends greatly on the sincerity of our friendship, not merely when we are at prayer but at all other times. Even where our friendship with our Lord is sincere, the nature of our prayer will depend also on personal temperament. This stage of prayer may last a long time for some souls; for others, it may not come at all or only for a time. Other developments are possible which may either succeed this pleasant phase or anticipate it altogether. Much, as we have said, depends on temperament and also on our knowledge of God.

Increasing knowledge of the Divine Person to whom we are speaking, and especially increasing advertence to his Divinity, may change the nature of our prayer. We begin to suspect the inadequacy of it all. We may even begin to feel that there is something of self-love in our prayer, that we are more interested in the consolations of God than in the God of consolations. We may perceive the lack of correspondence between our promises and our performance. Apart from all that, the limitations inherent in any human emotion, however good or holy, may manifest themselves. Pleasure cannot satisfy us. We were made for something more, and our emotional reaction becomes less and less. We may begin blindly to feel that the picture our imagination forms of the Person to whom we are speaking is quite inadequate, that there is a lot therein of our own creation, a projection of human desires and experiences. It is true that all we can desire or admire in some way reflects God and can be found in God. Yet

God himself is much more than his reflections and, whether we know it or not, it is God himself that we need and are seeking.

Considerations such as these may have a considerable effect on our prayer and may even cause us to lose all the facility and enjoyment we once found in it. We arrive at a state which was described in the last chapter as the Prayer of Stupidity; and there is a great temptation to give up prayer as a waste of time that could be better employed. This is a critical *pons asinorum* in our advance to union with God. We have to remember that it is with our *will*, aided of course by grace, that we are to pray, and that although our will needs the lead of the intellect to act, yet our intellect must rely on the dim light of faith to feed it, so that we need not be disturbed if everything seems dark and dreary.

It is very important to realize that at this stage we have to be content with doing very little at prayer, and to be convinced that we shall not improve things by a violent effort to replace our apparently useless attempts by some sort of discursive meditation. Our principal difficulty is to deal with distractions. In a more affective and devotional phase of prayer we can manage distractions either by replacing them with some pious thought, or else by leaving them there, while looking over their shoulder, so to speak, at something which will hold our attention. Now there is nothing with which to replace them and there is nothing to look at which will occupy our minds.

Possibly the best policy is to fall back on those fundamental acts which are at the basis of the whole spiritual life. This we do by enunciating gently, very gently, acts of faith, of hope and of charity, in a very quiet and simple fashion, making no violent efforts to 'feel' what we say. To these we can add, explicitly or implicitly, an act of adoration leading us to a willing acceptance of our helpless position and circumstances. Even if we achieve no more than this in our time of prayer, we may be quite satisfied. As far as actual praying goes there is little more that we can do.

Any remedy—if there be one—must be sought for elsewhere. Obviously one must consider the possibility that this 'failure' at prayer could be due to our own infidelity. In practice one need not worry if examination reveals nothing more definite than a general sense of not doing enough for God or being fervent enough. It is only when our examination reveals some definite infidelity, some deliberate determination to persevere in a habit which we know to be contrary to God's will, that special action is called for. Even here one must be careful not to be misled by unreasonable scruples or by an exaggerated notion of the physical mortifications demanded for progress in spirituality. The fourfold purity of heart, of conscience, of mind and of action upon which prayer depends is a matter we shall discuss later. Here we wish to point out some considerations, too often overlooked, which may help to encourage the man who has come up against a stone wall in prayer, and who is tempted to abandon all further efforts.

Before doing so, we should like to remind the reader that we are considering progress in prayer from the human side. All prayer, of course, is supernatural and depends on grace, but the working of ordinary grace does not do violence to natural development, and we have refrained from discussing what special developments God may initiate by altering the manner in which he treats the soul at prayer. We prefer to reserve that question—upon which there is a certain difference of opinion—for separate treatment later. What we wish to do now is to urge the priest to remember the doctrine of grace and of filial adoption, to remember what he is by grace: a son of God, participating in the divine nature, a man in whose soul the Blessed Trinity dwells —for his enjoyment and for his use! If that seems too strong, let us quote Hervé:[1] 'Deus, secundum donum gratiae sanctificantis, praesens est in anima, modo novo et omnino speciali, non solum quatenus infundit et conservat in nobis dona supernaturalia, sed etiam quatenus personaliter in nobis inhabitat, se praebens nobis ut objectum intimum, quasi experimentaliter cognoscibile, quo iam aliqualiter uti et frui possumus.' St. Thomas uses a similar expression in the *Summa*:[2] 'Illud solum habere dicimur quo libere possumus uti vel frui . . . Sed in dono gratiae gratum facientis Spiritus Sanctus habetur et inhabitat hominem.' And if one needs authority for connecting this doctrine with prayer, let us quote St. Paul: 'Likewise, the Spirit also helpeth our infirmity. For we know not what we should pray for as we ought; but the Spirit himself asketh for us with unspeakable groanings.'[3] And again: 'You have received the spirit of adoption of sons, whereby we cry: Abba (Father). For the Spirit himself giveth testimony to our spirit that we are sons of God.'[4] We must make use of this tremendous gift of God; we must have recourse to the Holy Ghost, for 'God hath sent the Spirit of his Son into your hearts crying: Abba, Father.'[5] Did not our Lord tell us: 'Thus shall you pray, Our Father'?

It would not seem unreasonable to suggest that the providential reason for our paralysis at prayer is to force us to pray not by nature but by grace, to pray not as mere human beings but as sons of God, participating in some mysterious and analogous way in his power of knowing and loving himself. In fact, our Lord's repeated instruction to pray in his name takes on a new significance in our present circumstances; we begin to glimpse some faint view of the depth of meaning in his exhortation: 'Abide in me: I am the vine; you the branches . . . Without me you can do nothing.'[6]

The failure of our own prayer is a blessing, for it forces us to fall back on the prayer of Christ; it forces us to unite ourselves with him, to identify ourselves with him, to offer up to the Father his prayer and his love, to pray by his Spirit, the Holy Ghost. As priests we never question the powers of consecrating and absolving given to us by the sacrament of Holy Orders. It would be well to take a similar view of the power of prayer and worship given to us by the sacrament of Baptism and by every other sacrament which we receive. It is true that we cannot have the certainty of faith about our being in the state of grace, but since we must be morally certain of it to exercise various sacerdotal functions, we can use the same conviction when we go to pray. Even if we are sinners, we are still marked out as sons of God, in whose regard he has revealed his attitude and interest by the parable of the prodigal son.

We must, then, unite ourselves to Christ by faith, by hope and by charity. All his merits and his Passion have been communicated to us in Baptism as if they were our very own.[7] Therefore our past sins or our present unworthiness need be no obstacle to our hope and confidence. In fact, our Saviour has made our weaknesses his own, and we should present them to the heavenly Father in his Son's name. Our own powerlessness does not matter; our Saviour is praying, is adoring, is loving, in our name. All we have to do is to abide in him, by faith, hope and charity. We must never forget that the life of grace on earth is a foreshadowing of the life of glory in heaven. And the life of glory is not merely a passive beholding of the Blessed Trinity, but an entry into, and a partaking in some extraordinary and created way in their life. This participation should begin by grace on earth.

This subject must wait for further discussion in a later chapter, but by way of a practical hint, we would suggest that priests should revise the grace tract, in a *modern* text book, and develop its teaching in more specialized works. Nothing better has been printed on the divine indwelling in souls than the Rev. Fr. Blowick's articles in *Pagan Missions* in the years 1946 and 1947. (Would that they were reprinted in a compact form!) A better understanding of this doctrine will make us realize the force of St. Paul's teaching that the Holy Ghost prays for us and within us. For we have received the spirit of adoption of sons whereby we cry: Abba, Father.[8] In our aridity we can still truly say, 'We are saved by hope.' And hoping for that which we do not see, we shall wait for it in patience, which has a perfect work. Then will the Spirit help our infirmity, for we know not what we should pray for as we ought, but the Spirit himself asketh for us. That is the beginning of the true life of prayer which should be the life of every priest.

[1] Vol. III, n. 54
[2] I, q. 43, art. 3
[3] Rom. VIII, 26
[4] Ibid. 15-16
[5] Gal. IV, 6
[6] John XV, 4-5
[7] Cf. *Summa* q. 69, art. 2
[8] Cf. Rom. VII, 15

CHAPTER SEVEN

PURITY OF INTENTION

WE cannot carry our discussion on prayer much further without considering how prayer depends upon the general state of one's spiritual life. Prayer is a meeting with God, in which we give expression, in speech or in silence, to our acceptance of his will, our intention to carry out his desires and our own desire for union with him. If there is not some degree of sincerity in our dispositions, our prayer is little better than a delusion. Obviously, then, our facility at prayer will depend to some extent upon our general dispositions and upon the degree to which those dispositions influence our daily life. There is, in fact, a parallel between our progress in prayer and our progress in what may be summed up as the purity of our life. The two are mutually dependent. An advance in one will generally produce an advance in the other; and there are certain stages when progress in prayer will become very difficult unless there is also progress in purity of life. However, lest the reader should be discouraged, let us hasten to add that although there is a proportion between the two the ratio varies much from one individual to another. It depends much upon temperament, training, circumstances, previous history and character; and of course it is still more dependent upon the type of grace given by God to the particular soul. Every one has his own special gift from God. One meets men of great fervour of life, whose prayer, apparently at any rate, is not of a high order. On the other hand, one also meets souls who have advanced considerably upon the path of prayer and who still have many failings, sometimes of a surprising seriousness. All that can be said is that no man should allow either the consciousness of his own miseries or the sight of his neighbour's fervour to discourage him. Even though one feels oneself to be far behind one's fellow-priests in holiness it does not follow that one may not aspire to advance in prayer. In fact there is hardly any better way of making up for lost time. Nor need it be thought that one must mortify oneself to a heroic degree to achieve progress in prayer; although it is true that any prudent effort to purify one's life will produce abundant fruit at prayer.

The purity of life of which there is question in regard to prayer is generally considered under four heads: purity of conscience, purity of heart, purity of mind and purity of action.

Purity of conscience has reference to our intention of avoiding deliberate sin. As it develops it will determine us to take measures to avoid being overcome by weakness or by habit. However, it is capable of many degrees, and in practice there is no use in gazing at the apparently dizzy heights of purity to which the saints have attained until one is completely discouraged at the prospect of having to accomplish such an appalling ascent. All that is required is that we decide to take that particular step upwards which lies immediately before us. The rest is God's business and will be provided for by his grace when the time comes. This work of purification of one's conscience is one in which grace plays an ever-increasing part, and there is no use in considering tomorrow's difficulties in the light of today's grace. In fact it is dangerous and discouraging. Common sense, the Psalmist, the first Pope and even God himself all insistently remind us: 'Cast your burden on the Lord . . . *Ipse faciet.*'

Purity of heart has a somewhat wider scope. It refers to our attachments and our interests and, to some extent, to our joys and sorrows. Obviously a deliberately willed attachment, which we know to be opposed to God's will and which we know will lead us to act against it, is incompatible with sincere friendship with our Lord. To have our own natural tastes and interests is however quite another matter, and although they will often provide matter for mortification, yet if they can be subordinated to our love of God, they can play a very useful part in our spiritual life. In fact, to our mind, it could be a very serious mistake for a priest to reject and oppose all such congenial 'attractions.' There are times of temptation when it is very helpful, even for the fervent, to have a harmless interest or recreation to which they can turn, relying upon their attraction for it to draw them out of their difficulty and to give them a breathing space. And in Ireland there is a widespread liability to periodic depression which can be an occasion of serious lapses for a priest who has no 'attractions' which can take him out of himself at such times. In practice one must distinguish sharply between inordinate attractions and those which are under proper control. The former, of course, must be opposed; the latter, however, have to be handled prudently and in many cases they are better left alone, at least until one has made further progress in union with our Lord.

Purity of mind has to do with the course of our thoughts. It is, of course, closely connected with purity of heart, for our mind tends to be occupied with that to which our heart is attached. A man who wishes to live in intimate friendship with our Lord cannot let his thoughts and his fantasies run riot. Even apart from avoiding sinful preoccupations, there is room for a measure of prudent self-control in this matter. In fact, it might be advisable for some of us to examine ourselves in regard to the usual course of our thoughts during the day. We may perhaps detect a tendency to live in our imagination, which, by the way, is the direct opposite of living a life of interior recollection in the spiritual sense. In fact the imagination can be a greater enemy to union with God than external distraction. But even if we are extroverted, we may find that certain things are constantly preoccupying our mind. Such a discovery, by making us seek for the cause of the preoccupation, may put us on the track of a major obstacle to our progress in divine union.

Purity of action is not altogether distinct from the other three divisions for it concerns the motives and desires which animate and dictate our actions. A good work done for a selfish motive is obviously not perfectly pleasing to God. Yet there is a legalistic mind which satisfies itself that it has fulfilled all justice in performing the daily duties of a pastoral charge without any advertence to the interior 'how' and 'why' of their performance. Prayer is not the only thing which God will reject because the heart is far from him. The true perspective in this matter can best be formed and maintained by a frequent reading of our Lord's address to his apostles at the Last Supper.

In practice, we would suggest to any priest who

desires to advance in his spiritual life a threefold attack
on this problem of purity of life. First would come the
question of habitual sin or of some habitual compromise in regard to one's clear obligations. If a short
examination reveals the existence of some constant
lapse of this sort, then the situation calls for a deliberate
and definite decision in regard to the future—a decision
which must be energetic enough to initiate measures to
remedy the fault and firm enough to persevere in the
amendment of one's shortcomings. Prudence of course
will avoid a too general assault on a number of failings
all at once. Where the enemy is manifold, the sound
policy is to divide and conquer. However, this particular
point is amply treated in ascetical literature.

The second suggestion is that we make a not-too-
casual survey of the customary course of our thoughts.
First of all, one should look out for any constant
inordinate preoccupation of one's mind, especially for
a habitual tendency to roam in forbidden fields or
along their borders. Even in imagination one must
always play the game according to the rules. Those
self-exalting day-dreams that are the refuge of an in-
feriority complex or the result of a self-centred ambition
may perhaps be excusable in the adolescent, but not
in the mind of the mature priest. Even where the
customary course of our thoughts runs on the works
by which we serve God, there is still room for a critical
enquiry lest concentration on the service of God should
exclude from our minds the God whom we serve.
The ideal to which we should tend is to have God—in
some way—habitually in our thoughts. To do this,
one might aim at the ideal of entertaining no deliberate
thought which we cannot share with our Lord. But
such an aim must be accompanied by a well-balanced

outlook in which the will of God is not distorted. For example, it would be fatal if we thought that we could not share our recreations or our pleasures with him who is our Friend. In this way an over strict, quasi-Jansenistic outlook can easily ruin our spiritual life. We must never forget that our Lord insisted that his yoke is easy and his burden light. He understands our needs and has compassion on our weakness. We must not think of him as a prying policeman anxious to catch us overlooking the letter of the law or as a dean of discipline intent on keeping us from every distraction. (It is extraordinary how much we transfer the memories of these two personages to him!) No! Our Lord is first of all our Saviour and we are his friends. He died to make us happy—praying that his joy might be in us and leaving us his peace.

The third suggestion we make is that each priest should try to find out what are the motives which habitually dominate his actions. This is, perhaps, the most important of all, and its importance increases the more exact a priest feels himself to be in the performance of his apostolic duties. We must always be on our guard lest the work which we commenced for the sake of God should be continued primarily for its own sake. When we examine the motives and zeal of those pursuing a career in secular activities we cannot deny the possibility that similar motives could assume charge of some of our ministerial work. Living among men whose lives are animated by the pursuit of power or of place, of pleasure or of possession, we priests should not too easily assume that we are immune from any infection of that sort. And such infection could, of course, have grave consequences. If a priest allowed advancement or preferment to become the main object of his work, he would no longer be serving God, he would be simply serving himself. And this could be done without departing externally from any of the conventional standards of the zealous priest. It might even produce a life of energetic activity which, since it is not possible for those in charge to assess the interior springs of such activity, might win official approval. For that reason we must be censors of our own motives and aims. Our Lord laid down the only principle of fruitful activity in the apostolate: to abide in him. If we do not abide in him, it is possible that our ministry may appear fruitful, but it is certain that the fruit is ours only in appearance. Its real author is some hidden soul who abides in the Vine in poverty of spirit, and who will be given the eternal credit for the fruit of his abiding therein, even though it seems to be the result of our labours. We are, of course, only pointing out the dangerous rocks to be avoided, but human nature is such that the avoiding of these hazards is secured only by constant vigilance.

There are, then, many possibilities of subtle self-seeking and merely human motives which can interfere with our priesthood. If we make our priesthood consist in the active work of the ministry, in preaching, in administration, in organization, in direction, in hearing confessions and guiding souls, there is a danger that we welcome or at least permit such motives to animate our work or to make it more energetic. Our very zeal for souls may welcome such motives as allies. The immediate effect of such a development is loss of purity of intention and a corresponding decrease in our union with Christ. That is serious enough, but still more serious is the effect on our general lives as priests. We become impatient with all those things that interfere with or lessen our success. Official orders or appointments that interfere with the development of our own methods or limit their application are resented. Work that does not suit our special talents may even be despised. The hundred-and-one happenings which should be accepted as manifestations of God's will are impatiently resented as enemies of our own ends.

Our own personal spiritual life suffers. The time given to attempts at mental prayer comes to be regarded as time wasted. Reading and reflection, if not completely given up, are used as a preparation for preaching and direction. At best, our own spiritual life is regarded as ancillary to the work of the ministry; at the worst, it is viewed as an accidental ornament in the life of a priest and eventually neglected as quite a useless one. These, of course, are only possibilities and things may never go so far. We may still regard trials and disappointments as something to be tolerated and offered up for souls. But we find it hard to embrace such things by preference as the best way of saving souls and as the real work of the priesthood. Yet—what is the lesson of our Lord's life?

For our Lord redeemed and saved the world on the Cross. It was by his Passion and his Death that he gave life to men; everything else centred on that. It was by his sufferings rather than by his activities, by what he permitted men to do to him rather than what he did externally to men, that his life-work was accomplished. If such a paradoxical mystery can be summed up in a phrase, that phrase would be St. Paul's assertion: 'Christ delivered himself.'

That is our vocation. Pius X puts it clearly. 'Est igitur nobis persona Christi gerenda.'[1] The same Holy Father insists on the need for a true interior reproduction of the life of Christ in our souls. 'Unum est quod hominem cum Deo conjungat . . . . vitae morumque sanctimonia . . . . Haec . . . . sacerdoti si desit, desunt ei omnia . . . . Sanctitas una nos efficit quales vocatio divina exposcit: homines videlicet mundo crucifixos et quibus mundus ipse sit crucifixus, homines in novitate vitae ambulantes, qui ut Paulus (2 Cor. vi.) monet, in laboribus, in vigiliis, in ieiuniis, in castitate, in scientia, in longanimitate, in suavitate, in Spiritu Sancto, in caritate non ficta, seipsos exhibent ut ministros Dei.'

We have, perhaps, drifted away from the direct discussion of our original topic of purity of intention and action. Yet the drift is not into irrelevancies. It is only in light of the cardinal principle of all fruitfulness, namely abiding in Christ, that we can see things in their true perspective. And it is only when one reads such authoritative statements of the need for sanctity and 'self-deliverance' in a priest that our insistence on the fourfold purity will not seem impractical idealism.

It is therefore in the complete oblation of ourselves at Mass in union with Christ, who delivered himself, that we shall find the solution of all the problems of our spititual life as well as those of our ministry. If we may use a phrase, unsuitable, perhaps in such a context but at least expressive in its brevity, we would say that our main object in the service of souls should be, not so much to 'deliver the goods' but rather, like our Divine Master and Friend, to deliver ourselves.

The proper discussion of this question must be reserved for further treatment. Here we only say that in this delivering of ourselves, in this purification of our motives and actions there must be prudence. If a man throws away all his natural motives and interests, he may find that his physical organism suffers. There is a physiological need for pleasure, for interest, for enthusiasm, as there is for food. Extremes must be avoided. One young priest, when told that if Christ were his all there would be no need for any recreation, made the quite logical retort that on the same basis of argument there would be no need for any dinner! A man will get the best out of himself only by adapting his way of life to the complex nature which he has to handle, but he must make sure that it is for God and not for himself that he is doing so. And as his complex nature changes through growth in grace, he may have to change his policy accordingly. He must at all times try to have a dominating supernatural motive. In fact he must make God and union with God the principal motive and aim of his whole activity. As we have said before, a frequent re-reading of our Lord's address to his apostles at the Last Supper is an excellent way of maintaining a true perspective, but sincerity in our offering when we say Mass is the secret of living in true accord with the mind of Christ.

[1] Letter to the Clergy, Aug. 4th 1908. Cf. I. E. R. 24 p. 527

CHAPTER EIGHT

PROGRESS IN PRAYER

In our last chapter, we have drawn attention to the connection between progress in prayer and the general fervour of a priest's life. In particular we drew attention to that fourfold purity of conscience, of heart, of mind and of action upon which the sincerity of prayer depends. Given some measure of this purity, prayer may be expected to develop. It is true there are books which leave one under the impression that there is no medium between discursive meditation in which reasoning plays the major part and a type of infused contemplation which is sometimes described as miraculous. This opinion we reject completely, and confidently assert that there is a progress and a development in prayer. All that we have written here and elsewhere[1] involves and explains this assertion. Meditation leads to affective prayer. Affective prayer tends to simplify itself as purity of life increases and friendship with our Lord develops. Eventually it may become a sheer loving attention to God's presence, in which very few words are used. This, however, may sooner or later be replaced by a state of complete aridity for which we borrowed the term 'Prayer of Stupidity'.

About the nature of these simplified and arid states of prayer and about their further development, there is room for considerable difference of opinion. Here we are not concerned with the theoretical issues involved. Our interest is in the practice of prayer by the priest and in the progress which he should expect. But before attempting to discuss this question, we must try to decide what is the normal vocation of a priest, as such, in regard to the spiritual life, since the whole question of prayer is closely bound up with that of general spiritual progress. Now it is true that the priesthood is not, canonically speaking, a 'state of perfection'. A priest, in virtue of his *state*, is not bound to tend to perfection as is a religious. But—again we must insist —a priest *is* bound to tend to perfection in virtue of his ordination and his office. As St. Thomas says: 'By Holy Orders a man is dedicated to the most august mysteries, wherein Christ himself is served in the Sacrament of the Altar; for this there is required a greater interior sanctity than is required for the religious state'.[2] 'Holy Orders requires holiness: but the religious state is a certain exercise to attain holiness; the load, therefore, of Orders requires walls already dried by holiness; but the burden of the religious state rather drys the walls—namely men—by removing from them the waters of their defects.'[3] We do not intend here to prove the thesis that a priest is called to holiness; we only assert the obligation and indicate its origin. St. Thomas is quite definite in tracing it back to the sacrament of Holy Orders. This is of great importance, because if the sacrament obliges us to become holy it also assures us the grace to do so. The character imprinted by ordination is considered to be a participation in the priesthood of Christ. This participation demands holiness. In the previous chapter we quoted Pius X: 'Est igitur nobis persona Christi gerenda.' May we

again recall his insistence that 'vitae morumque sanctimonia' are so necessary to the priest that if these are
wanting to him, 'desunt ei omnia' and further: 'Sanctitas
una nos efficit quales vocatio divina exposcit: homines
videlicet mundo crucifixos et quibus mundus ipse sit
crucifixus, homines in novitate vitae ambulantes'?[4]
The very fact that a priest consecrates in the first person
singular and offers sacrifice—the sacrifice of Christ
himself in which he is both Priest and Victim—should
be sufficient to indicate to what holiness a priest is
called. Our Lord himself summed it all up when he
said: 'You are the salt of the earth.'[5] How can men be
called to be the salt of the earth, without at the same
time being called to holiness?

If we labour the point it is because there is in this
matter a lot of misunderstanding, arising from the
statements of some writers discussing the priesthood as
a state; and also because in comparison with the life
of a religious, the life of the priest seems so beset with
obstacles to progress that one might well despair of
advance.

Yet priests are the salt of the earth. And in this
connection may we digress to hint at the special importance of the question at the present time. The most
essential need of the Church at the moment is the
development of a deep interior spiritual life among the
laity. They depend for this upon their priests. And it is
for the diocesan priest rather than for religious to
work out and teach the way to live a spiritual life in
the world. It is the secular priest who shares the layman's life and lives under similar conditions. The
difficulties are obvious but they are not insuperable.
And that is all the more evident since Pius XII recognized the Secular Institutes of men living in the world

and following their civil avocations as 'states of perfection'.[6] Members of such institutes have far fewer aids to holiness than a priest who says Mass and the Office, and administers the sacraments. So that there can be no doubt that it is both possible and of obligation for every priest to tend towards perfection.

That being so, we make no apology for discussing further advance in prayer as part of a practical programme for priests. And we can assure readers that we have seen ample evidence of God's willingness to be, in these critical times, more than usually generous with his gifts of grace to those who make any reasonable effort to prepare their souls for his mercy. And we speak of those whose circumstances seemed almost directly opposed to the development of spiritual fervour and an interior life.

A priest then—and it is the diocesan priest out in the world that we have particularly in view—has by his ordination and office acquired an obligation to be holy and a right to expect all the graces necessary to reach that holiness in those very circumstances, however unsuitable they may appear, in which he has to live and work. He has therefore—it seems to us—no right to say that progress in prayer is not for him, that it is something for monks and nuns but not for secular priests. Quite the contrary! No one, we believe, has as much right as he to look with confidence for the graces needed to live a life of prayer. No one needs it more than he does and hardly anyone (with the exception of the episcopate) is called by his state to higher perfection than that which a priest's office requires. That being so, let us face the question of progress in prayer.

In practice—whatever be the theory of the nature of development—progress in prayer sooner or later means

aridity, aridity prolonged and plentiful. Such aridity
may, of course, be due to unfaithfulness; it may be due
to a want of a sufficient degree of that fourfold purity
of which we have spoken. Bad health, too, may bring
it about for a time. Aridity does not necessarily mean
progress, but progress does definitely mean aridity.
(This, we may add, is written for your consolation!)

To decide what is to be done when one finds this
complete aridity at prayer, one must first investigate its
origins. An examination of conscience, aided perhaps
by consultation with a sympathetic, wise and experienced director, will either show us a cause for our
state in our infidelity or else reassure us that there is
no need to be anxious on that score. If we are at fault,
we must first remove the causes of our spiritual disease
and then return to our attempts to advance. If, however,
there is no obvious fault we may use the three tests
indicated by St. John of the Cross. The first is inability
to meditate. When we apply ourselves to prayer we can
produce no thoughts or ideas; all our powers, otherwise
quite vigorous, seem paralysed. God seems far away
and so remote that we cannot make contact with him.
Secondly, not merely is our mind inert but our heart is
also quite dry. Not only does it find no attraction
leading to God, no sentiments of fervour or devotion,
but it even experiences a sense of aversion and disgust.
The third sign is that there is a general sense of our
need of God and no peace can be found elsewhere. In
fact, if we could but see our innermost dispositions
we would realize that what we want is not thoughts
about God but God himself; we are not satisfied with
talking *to* him, we realize our need of union *with* him.
But all that is hidden and we cannot see it; we only
sense our paralysis and feel like a dumb animal in the

desert. This paralysis arises only in connection with God. With regard to creatures we are by no means powerless. In fact our imagination runs riot at prayer and we may even be strongly tempted to intoxicate ourselves with creatures or with work in order to escape from this emptiness. But there is a deep drawing of the will to God.

This is a roughly sketched picture of the state to which progress leads. On the way thither, the three symptoms may not be quite clearly present and the condition not so definitely established. But to try to return to meditation or affective prayer is not only useless: it is quite harmful, for it means turning back and refusing to co-operate with God's gifts of grace.

For one thing, God's grace is not using our imagination at all. This faculty is free to roam off on its own with a hundred and one distractions. There is no use in going after it to bring it back. To attend to it at all is to give up praying. The proper thing to do is either, so to speak, to look over the shoulders of the distractions as one does when a crowd is in the way at a match, or else to realize that these distractions are on the surface, as it were, while our prayer lies deeper. Such distractions do not interfere with this obscure type of prayer of faith; in fact, they are characteristic of it in certain phases. Again, there is no use in trying to think thoughts or ideas about God. Our mind is blank, for God's grace is directly concerned only with our wills, and it is with our wills that we must pray. This we do, as Fr. Piny writes, 'by *willing* to spend all the time of prayer in loving God, and in loving him more than ourselves; in *willing* to pray to God for the grace of charity; in *willing* to remain abandoned to the Divine Will. One must clearly understand that if we *will* to love God (abstracting from the part played by grace), by that very action we actually *do* love him; if, by a real act of the will, we *choose* to unite ourselves to the Will of him whom we love, or desire to love— by that very act of the will we immediately effect this union. Love is in truth nothing else but an act of the will.' Since all the grace that God is giving us in this obscure prayer is directed to our will there is little good in trying to use any other faculty. And what is given is given in such an obscure fashion and works so secretly that we can hardly perceive it even by reflection. We feel quite foolish at prayer and are almost certain that we are wasting our time. This is a feeling to which we must *never yield*. We can do nothing else with regard to prayer except to give up our attempt at prayer. To do this would be fatal. We must grimly resolve never to give up and still more grimly persevere in our attempt at prayer, such as it is. We are out in the desert. To turn back to the fleshpots is disastrous; we must keep on until we see the Promised Land, and *it has been promised*. 'Ask, and you shall receive; seek, and you shall find; knock and it will be opened unto you.'

What then are we to do? First of all, we must be reasonably sure that our failure at prayer is not due to laziness, tepidity or psychological depression. Here our confessor or our friends may help.

This precaution having been taken, we apply ourselves to our prayer as best we can. At the beginning of it a few lines of a book, a few familiar words, may help to get us started. But it must be clearly understood that, no matter how we start, we are not going to be able to continue either *thinking* or *talking*. When we have got to this stage where we cannot fix our thoughts on any subject at prayer, or where we cannot attempt to understand our words without feeling that we are ceasing to pray by doing so, then we are meant to cease thinking and to pray by faith with our will. There is no need to force acts. All must be done gently. Let acts come if they will in their own way without any excitement, strenuous effort or 'fervour'. They will probably be 'calm, simple, unmeaning and unfelt.' These are Dom Chapman's words[7] and the last two are the key words of the whole thing: '*Unmeaning and unfelt.*' There are going to be no feelings, that day is done. There is going to be little or no variety in our acts. These will generally be some expression of our need of God, even though God seems to mean nothing, to be miles away and quite heedless of us. Still we believe in him. And that is why we call it the prayer of faith. Readers will get great help at this period from a book by Fr. Ludoirc de Besse O.S.F.C., *The Science of Prayer*. And the classical reference is to St. Francis de Sales' example of the statue in his *Treatise on the Love of God*. We have to be content to remain like statues before our Lord and Master, quite satisfied to do so as long as we are pleasing to him.

Progress at this period is to be sought for in our general spiritual lives rather than at our times of prayer. Humility in particular is the virtue we require. As there are many wrong notions of this virtue we would suggest the reading of the chapter on humility in Dom Marmion's book, *Christ, the Ideal of the Monk*. His treatment of the subject is one of the best we know of, based as it is on St. Benedict's teaching which was adopted by St. Thomas. St. Benedict divided progress in interior humility into seven degrees, starting with obedience to the will of God and developing by increasing acceptance of the will of God and ever-deepening reverence for him. The fourth degree is 'to keep patience in the exercise of obedience, and not to lose it or depart from it, either because of the difficulty of the thing commanded or the injuries to which one may be subjected, according to what is said in the Scripture: He that shall persevere to the end, he shall be saved,[8] and again: Let thy heart take courage: and wait thou for the Lord.'[9] This, as we have mentioned above, has has been called the *Pons Asinorum* for those seeking God in the spiritual life.

It generally happens that at this period, when our prayer seems to go all wrong, other things begin to 'go wrong' also. There come various trials: difficulties with our neighbour, misunderstandings with our superiors, failures in our work, opposition to our plans, frustration of all our hopes. They may even be so severe as to seem to amount to genuine injustice. Even God seems to have let us down; at least we are no longer conscious of that providential co-operation with our plans and our progress that attached us so much to him. And the result is we begin to rebel, or at least to give up seeking him. We are not quite so enthusiastic about his service when it appears to hold so little hope for ourselves, so we let go and turn away instead of following the ideal of St. Benedict: 'In duris et contrariis rebus, vel irrogatis injuriis, tacita conscientia patientiam amplectans et sustinens.'

This is the critical point of the spiritual life. Our Lord has warned us that our Father, the good husbandman, will purge us that we may bear more fruit. He himself has insisted that we must be ready to deny ourselves and to take up our cross daily. And the Holy Spirit has given us the story of Job, which, we must realize, is full of meaning and significance for all who

seek God. With Job, we who have joyfully received
good things from the hands of God must be prepared
to accept less pleasing dispensations of his fatherly
providence with no less joy and gratitude. With St. Paul,
we have to learn to abound and to be in poverty. For
our poverty of spirit is our title to the kingdom of
heaven. As a preparation for union with God we must
learn by experience that we can do nothing without
him. This is the reason of our paralysis at prayer.
We pray henceforth by accepting our powerlessness
to pray. We pray by glorying gladly in our infirmity and
hoping with a sure hope against all hope that the power
of Christ will dwell in us.

Daily we must offer ourselves in the Mass in union
with him who is our Victim and who offers us up with
himself. And we must try to accept every detail of our
daily lot in the spirit of a victim in union with Christ
on the Cross, hoping to receive all things—even the
power to pray—from our Father in heaven. All this
is to be done in obscurity, without any consciousness
of our own acts. Yet we must persevere to the end. In
a word, we must do as the Psalmist bids us: 'Let thy
heart take courage: and wait thou for the Lord.' He
himself will come to save us.

[1] Cf. *Difficulties in Mental Prayer*
[2] *Summa* II-IIae. q. 184 art. 8
[3] Ibid. q. 189, 1 ad 3
[4] Cf. Letter to the Clergy, Aug. 4th 1908
[5] Matt. V, 13
[6] Cf. *Provida Mater Ecclesia*, 1947
[7] Cf. Appendix to his *Spiritual Letters*
[8] Matt. XXIV, 13
[9] Ps. XXVI, 14

CHAPTER NINE

UNION WITH CHRIST

MORE than once in these pages we have reminded our readers that, although the priesthood is not a *state of perfection* in the canonical sense, yet there is no doubt whatever that a priest is bound to tend to perfection in virtue of his ordination and his office. St. Thomas in the *Summa*[1] is quite definite about this, saying that in the priest, because of the most august mysteries to which he is dedicated, 'there is required greater interior sanctity than is required for the religious state.' Pius X was insistent on this point. In his very first Encyclical,[2] he summed up his policy in the words of St. Paul: 'Instaurare omnia in Christo . . . ut videlicet sit omnia in omnibus Christus'.[3] And, in order to achieve this purpose, he exhorts the hierarchy to make their first charge that of sanctifying the clergy: for Christ must first be formed in those who are chosen for the work of forming him in others. And the standard of holiness he sets for priests is significant. 'Qui tamen explere munus queant, nisi priores ipsi Christum induerint? Atque ita induerint, ut illud Apostoli eiusdem usurpare possint. "Vivo ego, iam non ego, vivit vero in me Christus . . . Mihi vivere Christus est."[4] ' He even quotes the exhortation of St. Paul:[5] 'Ut occurramus in virum perfectum, in mensuram aetatis plenitudinis

Christi', which, although addressed to all men, especially applies to the priest who, he writes, 'idcirco dicitur alter Christus, non una sane potestatis communicatione sed etiam imitatione factorum, qua expressam in se Christi imaginem praeferat.'

Let us note this double aspect of our union with Christ. It is the priest's great privilege to be an *alter Christus* by a share in his power. His work is our work; his strength is our strength. We sacrifice in his name, we absolve in his name, we preach and minister in his name. In all these works, it is his grace that gives us the power to perform our priestly functions. At times, perhaps, our humility is not deep enough to prevent us ascribing some of our priestly work to ourselves, but few of us are so mad as to forget that the principal part is played by God himself. The very magnitude of the task imposed upon us by our ministry of itself recalls to us the fact that we share in the power of Christ. But we are not so mindful of the other facet of the identification which makes each of us an *alter Christus*: namely, that to which the Pope refers when he writes, 'sed etiam imitatione factorum.' Elsewhere he has expressed his teaching in a lapidary formula: 'Est igitur nobis persona Christi gerenda.' We must in fact put on the mind of Christ and share his interior dispositions as much as, if not more than, his exterior deeds. And while the circumstances of our appointed work will limit the extent to which we can exercise our share in Christ's powers and actions, little except our own lack of good will and generosity can limit the degree to which he can reproduce in us his interior dispositions by his grace.

And this is what he requires of us. He has not called us servants; he has chosen us to be his friends. And the friendship he looks for is that which, according to Pius X, is characterized by a union of mind and heart, a sharing of sentiment and outlook, a community of purpose and effort. As the Pope writes: 'Quoniam vero idem velle idem nolle, ea demum firma amicitia est; tenemur ut amici, hoc sentire in nobis quod et in Christo Jesu, qui est sanctus, innocens, impollutus . . . . At maxime, ut ministri eius in praecellentissimo sacrificio, quod perenni virtute pro mundi vita innovatur, debemus ea animi conformatione uti, qua ille ad aram crucis seipsum obtulit hostiam immaculatam Deo.' In other words we have to unite ourselves to Christ our Victim as well as to Christ our High-Priest. Friendship with Christ will not be very deep or very sincere if it excludes a sharing of his sentiments in regard to suffering. But we need not be afraid of being generous with him, for he has assured us that his yoke is easy and his burden light.

We have quoted Pius X, not in order to convince the priest of his obligation to be holy, but to show him that it is both possible and practical for him to be holy, and that holiness for a priest consists in loving friendship with the Sacred Heart. In fact, it is part of a priest's vocation.

If we priests fail our Lord, this, I think, is the point at which we fail him. There is a tendency to feel that the most important thing we do for our Lord is the work of our ministry or rather the apparent success of that work. Friendship and love tend to be regarded as the ornament of a priestly life rather than as its essential purpose. Yet this is just the opposite of the truth. When our Lord was ordaining the apostles and giving them his last testament before his death, all his words were of love and union rather than of works and fruit-bearing. It is true they were being made apostles; it is true they were being sent forth to bear fruit. But their apostolate and their fruitfulness were to be the result of their union with Jesus. We priests cannot ponder too often or too deeply those mysterious words of our Lord at the last supper: 'Abide in me: and I in you. As the branch cannot bear fruit of itself, unless it abide in the vine, so neither can you, unless you abide in me. I am the Vine: you the branches. He that abideth in me, and I in him, the same beareth much fruit: for without me you can do nothing.'[6] Any fruit we bear in the ministry is the result of union with Christ, if not our own union, then someone else's. That in fact is where we priests can delude ourselves very seriously. Our ministry may be quite fruitful for souls, but the major part of the reward may go to someone else whose union with Christ brought down the grace that made our work fruitful. We should not forget the teaching of Pius XI with regard to the value of contemplative monasteries in the mission fields. Approving the Constitutions of the Carthusians, he wrote: 'It is easy to understand how they who arduously fulfil the duty of prayer and penance contribute more to the increase of the Church and the welfare of mankind than those who labour in the tilling of the Master's field. For unless the former drew down from heaven a shower of divine graces to water the field that is being tilled, the evangelical labourers would indeed reap from their toil a more scanty crop.'[7] The point about this principle is not that it glorifies the contemplative life at the expense of the diocesan clergy, but rather that it warns the apostolic labourer that he too must be a contemplative. If he does not make his interior life of prayer and sacrifice the mainspring of his apostolic labours, he runs the risk of finding that most of the merit for his successes has been awarded to someone else.

However, the merit and fruitfulness of our apostolic labours are not the most important consideration. It is still more important for us to ask ourselves are we giving our Lord what he wants form us. Are we giving him that for which he ordained us? Recent years have seen many accounts of communications from the Sacred Heart, some perhaps less authentic than others, but all agreeing on one point, namely, that our Lord is not satisfied with the return we priests are making for his love. He has chosen us to be his special friends. He has chosen us to share the joys and sorrows of his heart, to give him sympathy for his sorrow, love for his love. He has not chosen us because of any merit or talent of our own, but because of his own goodness and mercy. He has not chosen us for what we are, but for what he can make of us. Any good there is in us is there because of his love. Because he has first loved us he has shared everything with us. He shared with us his merits, his powers, his virtues, his priesthood. He even shared in the punishment of all our sins, for he cannot share in their guilt. He has taken all our debts on himself. He has chosen us to share in his work, not because he needed our co-operation, but because he wanted us to share in his reward, in his happiness in heaven. And the one thing he wants from us above all else is our personal love. Is he being disappointed?

Perhaps it is because of a misunderstanding on our part, a false humility, a Jansenistic reverence, an exaggerated fear, that we fail to give him the generous love of intimate friendship for which he chose us to be priests. Perhaps it is because of a 'legalistic' view of our duties, which tends to emphasize the external action rather than the interior disposition, which sees in our obligations the prescriptions of a penal code rather than the beseeching appeal of a divine Heart impatient for our love. We do not know our Lord. We do not know his love. We do not know the longings of his Sacred Heart.

It would seem that our Lord feels that we priests treat him as One far away, One known all too slightly, One in whom we have too little confidence. He wants us to rekindle our faith, love and confidence, and to live trustfully in his intimacy, loving and loved. He wants us priests to carry on his work of casting the fire of Divine love upon the earth, but he insists that we can do that only if we know him and love him as he longs to be loved. Instead it would seem that we have too little confidence in him, that we even avoid him. He would have us use greater intimacy and confidence in our dealings with him, uniting ourselves to him in our hearts where he is ever present as long as we are in the state of grace. Love must dominate our fears, and we must never forget that, above all else, he loves us. He chose us because of the love he has for us, but he is hurt by our failure to trust in that love when we realize our own miseries and our faults. We do not understand his heart. We do not realize that it is our very destitution and helplessness that move his mercy towards us. We do not realize that by acknowledging and accepting our poverty and misery, and then turning trustfully to him, we give him pleasure and glory far in excess of our offences. He loves us as we are. He knows our frailties. He knows we will fall again. He knows how little value can be set on our promises.

But he is quite prepared to save us and restore us each time after our falls if we but turn to him with humble confession and loving confidence. For above all he wants our union and intimacy with him. His delight is to be with us in our very hearts, to be sought there, to be loved there. He has chosen us for this very life of union with him, to comfort him and to make reparation for the sins of those who offend him.

He wants us priests to study his heart, to know and share its feelings, to do all we can to realize its desires. No one can recall his address to the apostles at the last supper without realizing how true all this is; and we must remember that every word there has a special message for each one of us who are his priests. Pius X has warned us that holiness of life is the only thing which makes us worthy priests. If we fail in this we fail in everything. Haec . . . . sacerdoti si desit, desunt ei omnia.[8]

We must, then, try to correspond fully with our vocation. No sense of our unworthiness or our incapacity, no consciousness of our coldness, our tepidity or even of our sinfulness should deter us from seeking intimate friendship with Jesus. It is our nothingness that he wants. The only foundation for his work in our souls is our incapacity, our misery, our futility. He will even accept our sins, for he is our Saviour, come to save us from our sins. Even our future sins will be no barrier to our present intimacy as long as they are not willed here and now. In fact the glory of his love is wonderfully shown in his choice of such unsuitable material for the masterpieces of his mercy. To let our shortcomings persuade us that we are not included in his invitation to intimate friendship is to forget completely the laws of the supernatural life. First of all that life is completely *super*-natural; it is not limited by the limitations of nature. Secondly, it is gratuitous; even where merited, it is only so because of a gratuitous promise of reward. But above all, the supernatural is a participation in the divine. So that when it is a question of returning our Lord's love, our natural ability to love does not enter into it; we have to receive from our Lord the very love by which we are to love him. That is why our human or personal limitations should never be allowed to interfere with our hopes of fulfilling our vocation to be the chosen friends of our Lord, or with our privilege of making reparation to his wounded heart. For it is from his own heart that we are to draw the means and the strength to be his friends and to make reparation to him. He himself symbolized this in the case of St. Margaret Mary when he exchanged hearts with her. He expressed it to her explicitly time and time again. His heart is the source of all our love and friendship for him. What we have to do is to learn to draw upon its treasures.

We must, then, first of all make the person of Jesus a living reality in our lives by frequently conversing with him, in our prayer, in our visits to the Blessed Sacrament, in our Stations of the Cross. We must keep him before our eyes by our reading and our remembering. Secondly, we must remove any obstacles to intimate friendship which there may be in our outlook or in our lives. Attachment to sin, exaggerated fear of suffering, over-strict notions of our obligations, could interfere with our generous giving of ourselves. In this connection some harm may have been done by wrong distinctions between the active and the contemplative life, between the ascetical and the mystical life. It is true that there are Orders especially organized for contemplation; it is true that there are special states of infused prayer which are not common. That does not mean that the active life has nothing to do with contemplation, or that the ascetical life does not imply an interior life of union with God. Actually, as far as priests are concerned, our own opinion is that their lives should, *par excellence*, be a combination of both the active and the contemplative lives; that for them those states of prayer which some writers call mystical, but which are by no means extraordinary, are quite attainable. That, perhaps, is a matter of opinion. But we think there can be no two opinions on this point, namely, that every priest, called by his priesthood to the active life of the apostolate, is by the very same priesthood still more urgently called to an interior life of union and intimate friendship with our Lord. If our Lord's words at the last supper mean anything, surely they mean that.

If a priest finds that mental prayer seems an imposition, if he finds that his spiritual life is one of mediocrity, if he finds that his words have no unction and his words but little fruit, perhaps it is because of his failure to realize this aspect of his vocation. On the other hand, our Lord himself assured some of his chosen souls that no other means are required to restore the mediocre and the tepid—even the sinful and the fallen—to their full fervour, than a confident appeal to his mercy and a loving intimacy with his Divine heart. He is our Saviour, we are his chosen friends, and his gifts are without repentance.

There is, then, no priest who cannot hope to give our Lord that love which he asks for and which he has merited. We have only to ask the Father for it in the name of his Son, our Redeemer, and we shall infallibly obtain it if we do not ask amiss. We have but to remind the Father of his Son's love for him and his merits which he has applied to us; to insist that what the Father does to us is done to his Son. And if more be needed, we have only to set before him the vocation which his Son has given to us to be his friends and the longing of that Son's heart for our love. And if that is not enough, let us go to Mary; let us tell her that we have no wine; that her Son has invited us to the wedding feast and we have no gift for him; that he has pleaded for our love and we have but cold, dry hearts to give him. Surely she will have compassion on her Divine Son if, *per impossibile*, she has not compassion on us. Here above all our poverty of spirit is our claim and our title to the riches of the kingdom of heaven. The Love of God for God, the Divine Spirit himself, is ours for the asking. Nothing is needed but our humble desire and our willingness to become what our Lord wants us to be: men after his own heart. This vocation makes no extraordinary demands on us for extreme penances or intense suffering. What our Lord looks for is that we love him in the ordinary things of our life; that we perform them in union with him, or rather, that we allow him to perform them in union with us. We priests should never let ourselves be persuaded that Jesus looks only to the cloister for love and reparation, expecting from us merely the service of our ministry. Far from it! Our ministry is only pleasing to him if it is the result of our love. We priests, let it be again repeated, are chosen to be his friends *par excellence*.

It is true that most priests have a special group of souls committed to their care. Too often we overlook our duty of prayer and mediation even in their regard.

But our charge goes further than any particular group. As priests we stand between God and *all* men. Our prayers and our penances are made on their behalf. But very often the work of our ministry is fruitless in regard to the group of souls committed to our charge. Then our only hope of fruitfulness is in our union with God. Where a priest does his work in union with Christ, abiding in him by lovingly doing his will, he will always bring forth fruit even though he may never see it in this life. Somewhere grace is brought down by his efforts. When we remember the wide tracts of the earth's surface where it is almost impossible for a priest to penetrate, we can realize how important this type of apostolic action may be today; and we may be consoled for the apparent waste of our efforts in tilling barren soil by the thought that if we do it in and with Christ, abiding in him, somewhere else all unknown to us, souls are being brought to the love of God. That is by no means the least important aspect of our vocation to abide in the Vine, by love and confidence. But this abiding in Christ is by far the most important aspect of our vocation as priests.

[1] Cf. II–IIae, q. 184, art 8; q. 189, art 1 ad 3
[2] *E Supremi Apostolatus*, Oct. 4th 1903
[3] Ephes. I, 10.; Coloss. III, 11
[4] Gal. II, 20; Phil. I, 21
[5] Ephes. IV, 3
[6] John XV, 4-5
[7] A.A.S. Oct. 15th 1924
[8] Cf. *Haerenti Animo*, Aug. 4th 1908

CHAPTER TEN

THE VIRTUE OF HUMILITY

In the previous chapter we were insistent that every
priest, called as he is by his priesthood to the active
life of the apostolate, is by that very priesthood still
more urgently called to an interior life of union and
intimate friendship with our Lord. In practice we think
that no priest will err in accepting this as a working
principle. It is perfectly true that a priest cannot
continue to be a friend of our Lord's or to be intimately united to him, if he neglects his apostolic obligations, but it does not always follow that a life of active
apostolate is accompanied by such friendship and
divine union. The importance of seeking for divine
union is, then, obvious. But how in practice are we to
find it?

Theoretically, perhaps, faith, hope and charity are
the virtues which we should exercise in order to achieve
this close union with our Lord. In practice, however,
humility has an importance that is in some ways pre-
eminent. For the whole of the supernatural economy
is based on grace: everything we achieve must come to
us from God. And God, as the Holy Spirit tells us,
'resisteth the proud and giveth grace to the humble.'[1]
God made the world, and God redeemed the world,
for his own glory. God associates us priests with him

in his saving and sanctifying work, but his own glory is still the fundamental motive of this work. It is true that he seeks his glory through his mercy. But the glory of his mercy is his own. He warns us: 'I am the Lord, this is my name; I will not give my glory to another.'[2] If we have not humility, we shall try to rob God of his glory and appropriate it to ourselves, and then God must resist us.

Let us, however, consider it from the point of view of friendship with our Lord. He has chosen us to be his friends, quite gratuitously. It is not for any goodness or value that is in us that he has chosen us. His motive is rather to give than to receive. He wants to make us sharers in his own happiness and it is in order that we may earn our share of his happiness that he makes us priests. He could do our work himself; he could use the ministry of the angels. But he has decided to co-opt us in sheer loving mercy without any claims on our part save that of poverty. It is his love that animates his choice and his generous bestowal of friendship. Even in human friendship, where one has chosen gratuitously and longs to do everything for the person one has chosen, what can cause so much pain and anguish as self-sufficiency? And in divine friendship the same is true. Our Lord knows our weakness, he knows our meanness, he knows our treachery, he knows our infidelity. All these he can heal and pardon. But self-sufficiency shuts the door on all his advances. He stands at the gate and knocks, and the self-sufficient will not open to him. Love calls for dependence, divine love especially so. Love wants to give, divine love most of all; but nothing can be given to the self-sufficient.

If a priest, then, asks what he is to do to meet the

demands of our Lord for his friendship, the best answer is that he should imitate St. Paul and glory gladly in his infirmities that the power of Christ may dwell in him.[3] Fr. Clerissac O.P. summed it up very neatly in the Introduction to his book, *The Mystery of the Church*, when he said: 'It is our emptiness and thirst that God needs, not our plenitude.' The realization of this truth is a great grace from God and it is one we priests should ask for, earnestly and insistently. Human reason and human experience may, perhaps, indicate to us the poverty of our own resources, but unless God gives us the grace we are not likely to relish our poverty and glory in our infirmities. Yet they are our most valuable assets for they are our title to divine union. 'Blessed are the poor in spirit: for theirs is the kingdom of heaven.'[4] Thomas à Kempis gives expression to our Lord's desire by putting the following words in his mouth: 'What more do I ask of thee than to try to give thyself up entirely to me? Whatever thou givest besides thyself is nothing to me: I seek not thy gift but thyself: just as thou couldst not be content without me, though thou hadst everything else: so nothing thou offerest can please me unless thou offerest me thyself . . . . Behold, I offered my whole self to the Father for thee, and have given my whole Body and Blood for thy food: that I might be all thine, and thou mightest be all and always mine. But if thou will stand upon thy own strength, and will not offer thyself freely to my will, thy offering is not perfect, nor will there be an entire union between us.'[5]

As usual, à Kempis sums it up in a phrase. If we 'stand upon our own strength' as he says, we cannot have complete union with our Lord. Jesus is not content to be merely our Partner, he insists on being our All.

It is, perhaps, an instinctive desire and striving for independence that is in many cases the cause of our failure to fulfil our vocation to be the friends of our Lord. In the natural order, the sons of men grow up from absolute dependence to an ever-increasing independence of their parents. In the supernatural order growth is quite different. In the earlier stages God's gifts endow us with a certain measure of independence. We feel we can stand, if not on our own strength, at least on the strength God has given us. To us it seems as if we had a reserve of power at our disposal, as if our priestly powers were our own. As we grow, however, our dependence becomes greater and greater. The more our union with Christ develops, the more complete becomes our dependence upon him. It is essential that we priests realize this. Otherwise all our striving will lead us away from God instead of bringing us to union with him, for our whole natural tendency is to try to develop our own competence and efficiency even in the supernatural order. We look forward to being able to handle any situation, to being strong enough to deal with any temptation, to being virtuous enough to perform all good works. True advance is quite different. One becomes more and more convinced of the essentially super-human nature of all supernatural works, whether in the service of souls or in our own sanctification. The inadequacy of our own power becomes more and more manifest. It is true, of course, that our confidence in God and our assurance of his co-operation are also ever-increasing, but we clearly realize that all that we have or do is the work of God rather than our own. In fact, our futility becomes so obvious that when souls come to us for help we hesitate to do more than promise to pray for them. Charity, and perhaps duty, demand that we make an effort to assist them, but our attempts are so clumsy and our words so foolish that we fly to our Lord to supply for our futility and failure. This is especially marked where there is question of direction of souls who are well advanced in the spiritual life. It sometimes seems that the grace we minister to them must be paid for by our own painful incompetence.

Yet this is typical of all our priestly life, in all its aspects. Divine union here below is to be sought for through and in Jesus Christ. And it is through and to Jesus as our *Saviour* that we must be united. The necessary disposition, then, on our part is the realization of our need of being *saved*. This is the very antithesis of self-sufficiency. And it makes clear to us how much of our striving to achieve union as a merited prize rather than as a merciful gift is wide of the mark. It also gives us great consolation and courage. For misery is the title to mercy and our short-comings are our claim to be saved. So that we cannot ever go to the throne of grace with more confidence than when we are most conscious of our own emptiness and futility. Even our sins and infidelities are no obstacle. We go to our Saviour to be saved from ourselves. And he himself will come and save us. This is the essential part of that self-denial upon which he insisted when he told us that we must deny ourselves and follow him. For he intends to replace our 'self' by himself. He is our Life and our All. If only we priests could grasp this principle, our whole life could be changed in a short time. But it means a complete change of outlook. Too many of us regard divine union and friendship with Jesus as something remote, something only to be achieved after a long laborious struggle in the spiritual life, something which is the reward for our fidelity and merit, and the crown of our strength and virtue. Nothing could be more misleading! The very commencement of the spiritual life involves divine union— a union so intimate that we are made partakers of the divine nature and become the dwelling-places of the Blessed Trinity. We are warned that we cannot have life unless we eat the Flesh of Christ and drink of his Blood; and this physical union with him, intimate as it is, is only a shadow and a sign of the much more intimate spiritual union with God which it produces in our souls. This union is the essential source of all Christian life. For us priests, especially, it is unquestionably true that we are called, and called most urgently, to live in intimate friendship with our Lord, not merely in the remote future, but here and now at this very moment. The friendship is not a reward for our virtue but a remedy for our sinfulness; it is not the result of our achievements but the essential means of our fruitfulness. We must, therefore, get rid of all that interferes with this friendship, and do all we can to promote it. In a word, we must be humble.

Perhaps the best way in practice to estimate our lack of humility is to consider the defects that this lack produces. And lest we be afraid to admit our shortcomings, let us consider these very defects in the apostles themselves. First of all, let us stand with the apostles when our Lord asks us all: 'What did you treat of in the way?'[6] Like them, probably, we shall have to hold our peace because it would be hard for us to deny that we were disputing, in one way or another, which of us should be the greatest. The desire to excel, to be successful, is usually evidence of self-seeking ambition. We feel we are self-sufficient and we

wish to have our sufficiency recognized and praised.
Our Lord's answer should warn us of our error; 'Amen,
I say to you, unless you be converted and become as
little children, you shall not enter into the kingdom
of heaven.'[7] Again, perhaps, we can find a fellowship
with the apostles in that scene where St. John reported
to our Lord: 'Master, we saw one casting out devils in
thy name, who followeth not us: and we forbade him.'[8]
How many diseases may lie behind such an attitude,
all different forms of self-seeking, jealousy at another's
success, a desire to monopolize for ourselves the glory
of the apostolate, stubborn attachment to our own
views, to our own traditions, to our own 'school'. Is
there any danger that we are tempted to hinder or
decry work done in the name of Christ for which we
ourselves are not going to obtain the credit?

Then, perhaps, we can find further fellowship with
the sons of thunder, who would command fire and
brimstone to come down from heaven and consume
those who opposed them or rejected their teaching.[9]
If so, we should be mindful of our Lord's rebuke:
'You know not of what spirit you are. The Son of
man came not to destroy souls, but to save.'[10] Patience
and mercy were characteristic of Christ; they must
also be characteristic of us if we are to be of the same
spirit as he is. These same sons of Zebedee may reveal
to us our own thoughts and desires when, on hearing
our Lord foretell his passion and death and ultimate
resurrection, they pleaded for seats on either hand in
his glory. Our Lord's answer applies to us also. It is
an invitation to drink the chalice that he drinks of and
to be baptized with the baptism wherewith he is
baptized.[11] And his warning to those who seek power
and authority may have its meaning for us if we wish

to be friends with him: 'Whosoever will be greater shall be your minister. And whosoever will be first among you shall be the servant of all. For the Son of man also is not come to be ministered unto but to minister, and to give his life for the redemption of many.'[12]

When we fail in our efforts, could he not often say to us, as well as to the apostles, that it is because of our unbelief, and when we succeed, do not our elation and self-satisfaction contrast with his words: 'When you have done all these things that are commanded you, say: we are unprofitable servants; we have done that which we ought to do.'?[13] How often do we regard ourselves as the one best fitted to deal with a certain situation or to handle a special type of soul! How often do we magnify ourselves in our thoughts, turning the gifts of God to our own glory, and flattering ourselves that we indeed are profitable servants, whose services are so valuable and almost necessary to our Master!

If we are to live in friendship with Jesus we must share his sentiments. We must, in fact, follow the precept of St. Paul: 'Let this mind be in you, which was also in Christ Jesus.'[14] Our Lord's whole aim was to 'empty' himself, to humble himself, to be obedient even unto death. In all things he was led by the Holy Spirit and lived for the glory of his Father. If we do not share his sentiments, if we are not of one mind with him, we are really against him. That is why he is so insistent that we, his disciples and his friends, must deny ourselves. No form of self-denial is so important as this complete renunciation of self, of self either as the centre of our life or as the source of our strength, a renunciation which is involved in true humility. In fact, it may be said that without this form of self-denial, all other forms are not merely delusions, but are even dangerous, for they can be the food of pride.

To acquire this humility, we must pray with sincerity and insistence. We must also cultivate the company of Jesus. He dwells in our hearts, he resides there to be our All. He is there as our Saviour. We must study him in the Scriptures; we must learn his ways—so meek and humble—by constant conversation with him. We must forget ourselves and depend on him. But we must, above all, have unlimited confidence in him. His mercy is infinite. There is nothing which he is not prepared to forgive. There is nothing which he is not prepared to remedy. There is nothing which he is not prepared to restore. He literally rejoices in being our Saviour. He is Love incarnate. His love rejoices in its omnipotent power to save us from ourselves. He rejoices with the whole heavenly court when, like the prodigal son, having wasted all our substance, we turn to him. He is on fire to make us his loving friends. We believe in him, but we must also believe in his infinite mercy and infinite love. He asks us for our love and that we should never doubt his love for us; above all he asks us priests that we should trust him and never, never doubt his mercy.

The virtue that opens the door to his love, and which is the foundation of our trust, is humility. It has a wonderful power of transmuting all our sins and debts into assets. Let us quote the words of Blessed Guerric, a disciple of St. Bernard, which are thus rendered and partly summarized by a modern Cistercian. 'Humility has a very special property of its own; it not only ensures that the other virtues are really virtues, but if any one of them is wanting, or is imperfect, humility, using that very deficiency, of itself repairs the deficiency. Therefore, if something seems to be lacking in any soul, it is lacking for no other reason than that the soul should be all the more perfect by its absence, for virtue is made perfect in infirmity. "Paul", saith the Lord, "my grace is sufficient for thee."[15] He for whom the grace of God is sufficient can be lacking in some particular grace, not only without serious loss, but even with no small gain, for that very defect and infirmity perfects virtue; and the very diminution of a certain grace only makes the greatest of all God's graces—namely, humility—present in a fuller measure and a more stable way. Far, then, O Lord, from thy servants let that grace be—whatever it may be—which can take away or lessen our grace in thy eyes (*gratiam tui*), by which, namely, although more pleasing in our own eyes, we become more hateful in thine. That is not grace, but wrath, for it is only fully fit to be given to those with whom thou art angry, in whose regard thou hast disposed such things, and that because of their simulation, thrusting them down at the very moment of their elevation and rightly crushing them even while they are raised on high. In order, therefore, that that grace alone, without which no one is loved by thee, may remain safe in our possession, let thy grace and favour either take away all other grace from us or else give us the grace of using all properly; so that having the grace by which we serve thee pleasingly with fear and reverence, we may earn the favour of the Giver through the grace of the gift, and that, growing in grace, we may be the more truly pleasing to thee.'

Humility, then, is all-important. And by humility we understand a disposition that tends to forget self completely and to remember only Christ. It is a great gift from God; in fact, in its higher stages, it seems to be an infused grace. But it is essential to divine union and friendship. So that we who are literally called to the wedding feast of the Lamb must have the wine of humility. And if we have no wine, we have but to turn to her whose humility prepared her to be the Mother of God and ask her, in the name of her Son, for that humility without which he cannot live in us. How can such a prayer be refused?

[1] James IV, 6
[2] Isaias XLII, 8
[3] Cf. 2 Cor. XII, 9
[4] Matt. V, 3
[5] *Imitation of Christ* IV, 8
[6] Mark IX, 32
[7] Matt. XVIII, 3
[8] Mark IX, 37
[9] Luke IX, 54
[10] Ibid.
[11] Cf. Mark X, 35 *et seq.*
[12] Ibid.
[13] Luke XVII, 10
[14] Phil. II, 5
[15] 2 Cor. XII, 9

CHAPTER ELEVEN

PROGRESS IN HUMILITY

IT is essential that anyone who wishes to succeed in the spiritual life should have a proper appreciation of the importance of humility. Very often humility is regarded as one of a number of virtues which would be desirable ornaments for one's soul but not absolutely essential. Sometimes humility is misunderstood and is regarded as demanding that a man deny or at least decry his own abilities and gifts, even to the extent of denying all that God has wrought in his soul. Both views are mistaken; for humility is an essential virtue which is so powerful that where it is present all else is added unto it, so that we may truly call it the one thing necessary; and it is based fundamentally on truth, the truth of what we are, of what God is and of what he has done for us. She who excelled all other human creatures in humility could exult in the knowledge that God had done great things for her. So important is this virtue, and so sufficent, that we feel bound to discuss it at some length despite the risk of repeating what we have already written and of wearying our readers with fundamental considerations.

Lest someone, knowing of the primacy of charity in the spiritual order and of the capital place given to it by St. Paul, should feel that we are exaggerating the importance of humility, let us quote St. Augustine on the subject. He writes: 'Ipsa est perfectio nostra, humilitas', and again: 'Universa disciplina christiana docet humilitatem qua et acquirat et custodiat charitatem', 'Nihil excelsius via charitatis et non in illa ambulant nisi humiles.'[1] It is precisely because charity is of primary importance that humility is so essential; for charity is the gift of God, and God will give his grace only to the humble. By the very law of his being he must resist the proud; for the proud assume to themselves the glory that belongs to God, and God cannot give his glory to another. What then is humility?

We can hardly find a better answer than that given by Dom Belorgey in his book, *L'humilité Bénédictine*, 'Humility', he writes, 'is the truth about our relations with God, recognized by our intelligence, accepted by our will and realized in our whole life.' (If this were to be amended in any way, we would insert the adverb 'lovingly' before each verb). This concept of humility is of special importance and significance for the priest. The priest's principal duty is to offer sacrifice to God; to acknowledge by a most sacred and solemn rite our relations with God and to profess publicly his complete acceptance of all that those relations entail. Each time a priest celebrates Mass, he makes public profession of these sentiments and associates himself with the dispositions which animated our Lord Jesus Christ in his sacrifice on Calvary. Obviously, humility, as we have just described it, is in perfect harmony with these dispositions and, as we shall see, sums them all up. Humility, then, is the fulfilment of that fundamental obligation of worship which the first of God's commandments lays upon us, a fulfilment which has an intrinsic value of its own in God's sight quite apart from any fruit or effects which it may produce elsewhere. We are inclined to forget that acts of the virtue of religion have a value of their own even though they have no apparent usefulness in our ministry. Our primary duty is the direct service of God; to love and serve our fellow men is only a secondary duty and a derivation of the first. Humility, then, must not be evaluated by its usefulness, even though in practice it can be the source of a most fruitful ministry. Its great value is that it puts us in our proper place in relation to God, and determines correctly our attitude to him. What is this attitude?

St. Thomas answers the question in the *Summa*:[2] 'Per sacrificia repraesentabatur ordinatio mentis in Deo. Ad rectam autem ordinationem mentis in Deum pertinet quod omnia quae homo habet recognoscat a Deo tamquam a primo principio, et ordinet in Deum tanquam in ultimum finem.' There we have it. All that we have is from God and must be ordained to God. And the Saint hammers it out in various places. God is our first beginning, the first principle of all we do, our supreme good and final end, by whom alone we can be made happy. This is dry doctrine, wearyingly familiar and dull. But look at its implications. It means that, having submitted ourselves to God and recognized him as the power behind all that we do, we then must admit that there is nothing he wills us to do that is outside that power. And having recognized him as our last end, we immediately see that we are called to intimate union with him, *and that all his power is at our disposal to effect that union*. Why,—to use a modern phrase, more expressive than elegant—it 'stands out a mile' in the Mass. Immediately after we offer sacrifice God gives us the Body and Blood of his Son as the food of our souls in order that we may be one with him. St. John Chrysostom condenses it into a marvellous phrase: 'ut unum quid simus.' That is why we need never be afraid of humility or reluctant to admit our lowliness in God's sight. Our very poverty of spirit is our title to the Kingdom of heaven. The Scripture tells us that God exalts the humble. One is almost tempted to say that humility itself exalts them!

Perhaps the close connection between humility and confidence may become apparent in this view of things. Recognition of our absolute dependence on God, so far from depressing us and crushing us, should, on the contrary, make us optimistic and courageous. For if God be with us what does it matter who is against us? If God is our strength (and he has said so himself) what can prevent our attaining all that he wills for us? And if God is our last end, is not union with him the supreme purpose of his will? It is significant that when our Lord was instituting the sacrifice of the Mass, he himself sounded and stressed this note of union. 'That they may all be one, as thou, Father, in me, and I in thee; that they also may be one in us . . . that they may be one, as we also are one. I in them, and thou in me: that they may be made perfect in one ... that the love wherewith thou hast loved me may be in them and I in them.'[3] This insistence on divine union becomes all the more significant when we recall the words spoken earlier in this discourse[4]: 'Without me you can do nothing.' It is precisely because we can do nothing of ourselves that we must abide in the Vine and put all our hopes in him who calls us to such intimate union.

Humility is but the recognition and willing acceptance of this fact. It means of course a life of ever-increasing dependence on God, but it also means a life of ever-increasing strength, confidence and joy. It means an entirely new appreciation of the great truth that all things work together for good to them that love God, and a joyous acceptance of our vocation to glory in our infirmities.

As a monk living by the rule of St. Benedict, I am rather loath to cite monastic principles of St. Benedict's teaching in support of this thesis, lest I seem to be led by personal preference and piety to apply to the secular clergy something which is intended only for the monastic life. Despite that danger, I think it will be useful to discuss St. Benedict's teaching on the point. St. Benedict lived in the fifth century when the doctrine of the apostolic age was still fresh in the Church and when it had not yet been adapted or developed to suit special needs and cases. In fact St. Benedict was legislating for men who wished to be perfect Christians in the shelter of the cloister. He proposes very little spiritual teaching except on humility. In his discussion of the twelve degrees of the ladder of humility he reveals his view of that virtue. He bases humility on the practice of the presence of God. 'The first degree of humility is always to have the fear of God before our eyes, never forgetting but always remembering what he has commanded.' He develops his teaching to include in this degree constant meditation on the abyss into which those fall who despise God, and 'on the eternal life prepared for those who fear him.' This leads to a continual guard against sins and vices, which is achieved by reflecting that the eyes of God are ever upon us, that all our actions, and even our desires, lie open to his view. The second degree of humility is 'that a person love not his own will, nor seek the gratification of his own desires, but shape all his actions according to those words of our Lord: I came not to do my own will but the will of him that sent me.' These two degrees of humility cover the conversion of a man from a life of sin (or perhaps the avoidance of sin from the beginning) and a subsequent advance to realize the importance of God's will. The passing of these two degrees may be regarded as the preliminary steps which have led us into the priesthood or into religion. The next degree is worded in a way suitable to the religious life, but it only adapts to it a principle which applies also to the life of a priest. 'The third degree of humility is for a monk to submit himself with all obedience to his superior for the love of God after the example of Jesus Christ of whom the Apostle saith: "He humbled himself becoming obedient unto death".' There is an important advance here, for it accepts the principle that God's will is shown to us by men, in whose divine authority we must believe and whom we should obey for love. The role of faith and charity is stressed and the example of our Lord takes a more important place. But the next degree is the testing-place of the spiritual life to which we have referred before, and which is the stumbling stone where many come to grief and failure in their quest for God. 'The fourth degree of humility is to keep patience in the exercise of obedience, and not to lose it or depart from it, either because of the difficulty of the thing commanded or the injuries to which one may be subjected, agreeably to what is said in scripture: "He that shall persevere to the end, he shall be saved",[5] and again: "Let thy heart take courage and wait thou for the Lord".[6]'

This is where most of us fail to carry out the sacrifice we make of ourselves at Mass. St. Benedict indicates one source of our failure when he quotes scripture to justify our subjection to human authority with all its limitations and mistakes: 'Thou hast set men over our heads.'[7] When we notice the human element in the men who rule us, or in the neighbours who try us, or in the mistakes and misfortunes that cause us so much trouble, we cease to take a supernatural view of things, we set aside our faith and we lose our patience and submission. This is a fatal error. St. Benedict exhorts us in the words of the scripture: 'Take courage and wait thou for the Lord.'[8] This is most important, because it is a reminder that God himself will come to aid us if we but wait for him as he has so often asked us to do. The saint goes on to develop his doctrine in terms that are very applicable to priests who, sharing our Lord's priesthood, should also be prepared to share his sufferings and patience as a Victim. He writes: 'The scripture furthermore teaches us that the faithful servant ought to suffer all things, however repugnant, for the love of his Lord, saying in the person of those who thus suffer: "For we suffer death all the day long: we are counted as sheep for the slaughter.".'[9] And he expects us to rejoice and to say: 'But in all these things we overcome because of him that hath loved us.'[10]

Let no reader say that this is for monks but not for secular priests. Are not priests the chosen *friends* of our Lord? Are they not chosen to be fellow victims with him just as they are priests with him? Are they not called to abide in the Vine that they may bear fruit? Are they not to be 'purged' that they may bring forth more fruit? To surmount this degree of humility, we priests may have to make radical adjustments in our outlook on our vocation and on our work. The time comes sooner or later when obstacles permitted by

Providence, and even seeming to come from the hand of superiors, may interfere with the work which we regard as our special vocation. A new appointment, a change of duty, a removal of some help or some such thing, can frustrate all our hopes and ambitions. And we fondly imagine that we are being prevented from doing God's work—that, in fact, we are being prevented from doing God's will by God's will itself! For everything that happens, happens to us according to his will. We forget that God's plan is of a piece. We forget that God has warned us that we are to be purged. We fail to realize that we are being invited to go up higher at the banquet of his love. We forget that, like our Master, it behoves us to suffer these things and so enter into our glory.

Mention has just been made of some of the events which may interfere with our patient submission to God's providence. Those mentioned are of course quite minor ones. St. Benedict's principle applies to a much wider field. It would cover such trials as those of the purifying 'nights' of which St. John of the Cross speaks, and would even extend to such sufferings as those of concentration camps which seem to be part of the sacerdotal vocation of so many of today's priests. The essential point underlying his doctrine is that as we cease to make ourselves the centre of our own lives and realize the completeness of God's claim on our devotion to him, we become more and more generous in our abandonment to his will, and more and more closely resemble our model and Master, Jesus Christ.

Pride is that disposition of mind and heart which makes self the principle of all our own excellence. We tend to regard our excellence as of our own making or meriting; we regard holiness and perfection as due to us; and we tend to make our own excellence our final end and purpose. Humility, on the contrary, although it does not deny the excellence of what God has done and will yet do for us, refers everything to God. This is its connection with sacrifice, for in the offering of sacrifices, according to St. Thomas, man avows that God is the first principle of the creation of all things, and the last end to which all must be related.[11] Humility establishes us perfectly in these dispositions, which should animate our daily celebration of the Mass.

Humility and confidence are inseparable. Very often we have no confidence because we are not humble. But sometimes we fail to become humble because we have not enough confidence. We do not realize that God is more anxious about, and more capable of, making us happy and holy than we ourselves are. We hang on to ourselves as a drowning man clutches at a straw, because we cannot or will not trust the ocean of God's mercy to support us. We are, in fact, like the apostles, 'men of little faith.' And the very same fear prevents us from being generous in our sacrifice. We forget the teaching of St. Augustine and St. Thomas: 'True sacrifice is every work that is done in order that we may cleave to God in a holy union, who is the final good by which alone we can be made truly happy.' If we but knew the gift of God, we would fly from the poverty of our own apparent riches and cleave to the apparent emptiness of the all-satisfying God.

St. Benedict completes the ladder of interior humility in the next three degrees. The fifth degree refers to our need of revealing our interior life to a competent guide who can represent God, for the Saint says: 'To this are we exhorted by the scripture in these words: "Commit thy way to the Lord, and trust in him".[12] In doing so we obtain pardon, we obtain light, and we obtain strength. The sixth degree asks us to be content with the poverty and abjection that may fall to our lot, whether interior or exterior, looking upon ourselves as unworthy servants, saying: 'I have been brought to nothing, and I knew it not: I am become as a beast of burden before thee, and I am always with thee.'[13] The seventh degree brings us to the height of interior humility where we sincerely speak and think of ourselves as the lowest of all—'a worm and no man, the reproach of men and the outcast of the people.' This appreciation of and joy in our own nothingness would seem to mean infused grace and light; it must be absolutely sincere, proceeding from an inmost conviction without the slightest trace of affectation.

The next five degrees are merely the external expression of our interior dispositions, whereby we avoid singularity and observe modesty in our speech and bearing, not being self-assertive, tending rather to be silent than to speak. When the height of this ladder is reached, St. Benedict promises us that we shall then 'attain to that perfect love of God which casteth out fear, whereby all that we dreaded so much at the outset, we shall begin to do without any labour—naturally, as it were, and by habit, not now through the fear of hell, but for the love of Christ, and because of the delight that attends the practice of virtue.'

To imagine that, however suitable this may be for monks, it seems quite outside the vocation and scope of the secular clergy would be a complete error. For the priest, by his office as priest, is called to the closest possible union with God, which means that he is called to climb this ladder of humility, there being no other way that leads to God.

In this chapter we have not been able to discuss the practice of humility in detail; but the broad outline has an importance of its own. And its importance increases in the case of secular priests. To the first secular priests our Lord himself said: 'Unless you be converted and become as little children, you shall not enter the kingdom of heaven.'[14] And God has since sent us, in the person of St. Thérèse of Lisieux, a living model of humility to recall us to the true notion of sanctity and perfection. The allocution of Pope Benedict XV on the occasion of her beatification is really a commentary on the text which we have just quoted. The Holy Father insisted that her way of spiritual childhood was meant for *all*, even for converted sinners. It is the way *par excellence* for us priests, both because of our personal vocation to sanctity and because of our official responsibility for the worship of God and for his glory. Let us pray, then, to Mary, whose humility made her worthy to be the Mother of God, to show us this way of sanctity and divine union and to obtain for us those special graces by which we can leave our self and cleave to God as our all.

[1] *In Ps.* 130, 14; *De Virg.* 31; *In Ps.* 141, 7
[2] I-IIae, q. 102, art. 3
[3] Cf. John XVII, 21, 23, 26
[4] XV, 5
[5] Matt. XXIV, 13
[6] Ps. XXVI, 14
[7] Ps. LXV, 12
[8] Ps. XXVI, 14
[9] Ps. XLIII, 22
[10] Rom. VIII, 37
[11] II-IIae, q. 102, art. 3
[12] Ps. XXXVI, 5
[13] Ps. LXXII, 22-23
[14] Matt. XVIII, 3

CHAPTER TWELVE

SPIRITUAL CHILDHOOD

THERE are few safer sources of doctrine than papal documents. And when to the significance already implied by beatification, such papal documents add that of an insistent emphasis on the universal application of the example and teaching of a particular saint, it would be folly to overlook their importance. It is generally admitted that the sanctification and the example of St. Thérèse of Lisieux were definitely designed by Providence to draw attention to the true way to holiness and to remind us of what holiness essentially requires. This general belief is in perfect harmony with the explicit teaching of Pope Benedict XV. His address on the occasion of the decree[1] on the heroic virtues of the now canonized St. Thérèse is of the utmost importance for the spiritual life of all men, and especially so in the case of all priests. Having summed up the saint's spirituality in the phrase 'spiritual childhood', the Holy Father proceeds: 'There lies the secret of sanctity . . . for all the faithful scattered over the whole world! . . . Her example', he hopes, 'will be the means of swelling the ranks of perfect Christians . . . wherever the children of the Catholic Church are to be found.' These striking words make it impossible for us to refuse to study her teaching and to apply it to ourselves. In order that we might do so the Holy Father went on to explain what he meant by spiritual childhood. Citing the example of a child's reliance on and confidence in its parents, he teaches that 'in the same way spiritual childhood is the outgrowth of trust in God and complete abandonment to him.' And he continues: 'It will not be out of place to enumerate the qualities of this spiritual childhood, both as regards what it omits and what it includes. It knows nothing of self-pride, or the thought of being able to attain by purely natural means a supernatural end, or those spurious notions of self-reliance in the hour of danger and temptation. On the other hand, it presupposes a lively faith in the existence of God, a practical homage to his power and mercy, a confident recourse to the Providence of him who alone can give us grace to avoid evil and to seek good.' And having thus summarized the essentials of this teaching, he adds the very grave statement: 'Our Lord Jesus Christ pointed to it as a necessary condition for obtaining eternal life.' These words alone justify our insistence here upon our thesis, for it is not merely a question of perfection, but of salvation itself! We must therefore listen further to the Holy Father.

He continues by referring to the incident in St. Matthew's Gospel where our Lord took a little child as a model and said to his disciples: 'Amen I say to you, unless you be converted and become as little children, you shall not enter the kingdom of heaven.'[2] 'Suffer the little children to come unto me . . . for of such is the kingdom of God. Amen I say to you, whosoever shall not receive the kingdom of God as a little child shall not enter into it.'[3] And the Holy Father continues:—'It is of great importance to note the force

of the language used by our Divine Lord. The Son
of God was not content with merely stating that the
Kingdom of heaven was for children: "Talium est enim
regnum coelorum", or that whosoever should become as
a little child would be greatest in the Kingdom of heaven;
but he even went so far as to exclude from his Kingdom
those who did not become as little children.' And
commenting on the various means used by our Lord to
impress this lesson on the minds of his hearers, the
Holy Father insists: 'From this we must conclude that
it was the Divine Master's express desire that his
disciples should see in the way of spiritual childhood
the path which could lead them to eternal life. In face
of this insistent and forcible teaching of our Lord, it
would surely not be possible to find a soul who could
hesitate in entering this way of confidence and self-
surrender, all the more so, to repeat our own words,
because our Divine Lord, not only in a general manner,
but also by a concrete example, declared this way of
life to be absolutely essential, even in the case of those
who have lost the innocence of their childhood. There
are some who try to persuade themselves that the way
of trust and abandonment to God is the exclusive
privilege of those souls whose baptismal robe has remained unsullied by sin. They are unable to reconcile
the idea of spiritual childhood with the loss of their
innocence. But do not the words of the Divine Master,
"unless ye be converted and become as little children",
indicate the necessity of a change? "Unless ye be converted" suggests a transformation which the disciples of
Jesus had to undergo in order to become children once
again; and who should become a child again, if not he
who is no longer one?' And the Holy Father continues
his explanation showing that our Lord's words indicate

an 'obligation to labour to regain the lost qualities of childhood.' And since there is no question of resuming either the outward appearance or feebleness of the state of infancy, the Pope sees here 'a counsel given to those who have attained maturity to return to the practices of the virtues associated with spiritual childhood.'

This long quotation is only excused by the need of establishing the papal endorsement of the doctrine of spiritual childhood. It is a doctrine which takes on a very special significance when we associate it with the teaching of the apostles in regard to the effects of baptism, by which we become the adopted sons of God, participating in the divine nature and being in all things dependent on him for every movement of life in our souls. Childhood in the supernatural order is nothing make-believe or far-fetched. It is the fundamental fact of the supernatural life. And it is only by spiritual childhood that we can live in true harmony with our nature and our dignity as sons of God.

Spiritual childhood includes three important virtues: humility of heart, poverty of spirit and unbounded confidence. We have been treating of humility in the previous chapters. To what we have already said let us add St. Thérèse's comment. 'To be little means not attributing to self the virtues one practises, believing oneself incapable of anything; it means recognizing that the good God places this treasure of virtue in the hand of the little child to be used by him when he has need of it; but always it is God's treasure. In fine, it means not being discouraged by our faults, for children fall often, but are too small to do themselves much harm.' For us priests this teaching applies not only to our own personal lives, but also to all the powers and graces we have as priests. Too often, although we do admit our limitations, we credit ourselves with something of our own. When serious obstacles arise in our path, then we are discouraged; the reason is that we have trusted, not in God, but in ourselves. Our proper attitude should be to lay aside any sense of our own self-sufficiency and to expect every necessary grace and strength from God. This of course means a life of complete dependence on God.

Often we are forced to admit our insufficiency. Our incapacity and our futility are only too obvious. But even then we only admit the truth to resent it. This is where we fail. True humility, true poverty of spirit, true love of our Lord rejoices in its poverty and exults in such complete dependence on God. Grace will come to such a soul in abundance when it is needed—but there must be no piling up of reserves, no proprietorship. One has to wait for each day and each deed for the necessary help to arrive. And when it does arrive, we must not make it ours: all is on loan. This poverty of spirit is not a passing phase. We have to be prepared to be poor all our lives. This is impossible if we have not proper confidence in God.

Too often our confidence in God is based on an illusory sense of our own merits. But true theological hope is based on the goodness of God, who is sufficiently good to overlook our lack of merit, and to be infinitely merciful to our poverty and nothingness. When a man realizes this truth, which is one of the most fundamental of all the truths of the spiritual life, he feels an urge to strip himself completely of all pretended possessions for it is when we are poor in ourselves that we are most rich in God. And such souls cannot hope too much in God. St. John of the Cross—a Doctor of the Church whom no one has ever accused of being lax—insists: 'From the good God we obtain all that we hope for.'

In fact, part of the proper office for the octave of the feast of St. Thérèse of Lisieux is taken from St. John of the Cross and bears out all we have said. The following teaching of the saint is quoted by the Church in the lessons for the second day of the octave:

'The greater the things God wills to give us, the more he increases our desires, even so as to make a void in the soul, in order to fill it with his good things. Firm hope is all-powerful to touch and vanquish the heart of God; and to attain to the union of love, the soul must walk relying on nothing but hope in God alone, without which it will be unable to obtain anything. The hope of a soul which ceaselessly turns towards him is so acceptable to God that it may truly be said that the soul obtains whatever it hopes for.'

Lest the reader should think that we are getting far away from the life of the secular clergy, let us quote from a letter of Pius XI to Fr. Fray, the superior of the French seminary in Rome:[4] 'The Teresian spirituality cannot be counselled strongly enough to souls, and especially to the souls of priests. It expresses the foundation of the Gospel. Its dominant note is simplicity in renunciation and entire sacrifice to love. And today more than ever the priest should give himself without reserve, without restriction, to the cause of God and the Church.' Thus encouraged, let us presume to put before the secular clergy another quotation from St. John of the Cross, also cited in the office of St. Thérèse's octave:

'It is of the highest importance that the soul exercise itself constantly in the labours of love, in order that, being rapidly consummated, it may not be retarded by anything of earth but quickly come thither where it will behold its God face to face. The smallest act of pure love is more precious in the eyes of God, and more profitable to the Church, than all other works put together. Without love all our works, all our labours, are as nothing before God, for he holds as acceptable only our love. Wherefore the soul which is aglow with this perfect love is named the Spouse of the Son of God, and appears to us as raised to a footing of equality with him, because their mutual affection renders all common between them. Enkindled by this love, the soul desires neither wages nor reward. Its will is to lose all and sacrifice itself without desiring to gain aught for itself, so that it may please Jesus. Happy the soul that loves! The Lord becomes, as it were, its prisoner, and holds himself ready to fulfil all its desires. Love is repaid only by love.'

No reader need be surprised at this sudden leap from the depths of childlike humility to the ardent heights of divine love. The vocation of every Christian is to love God with his whole heart and his whole soul. One might even say that his vocation is to love God with the love with which God loves himself. And the teaching of all Christian time, coming down from our Lord himself through his apostles, re-echoed by St. Benedict, by St. Thomas, by St. John of the Cross, by St. Thérèse, is that the way to the heights of divine love is by the path down into the depths of humility. To gain life we have to lose our own. To put on Christ, we have to deny ourselves. To let God act freely in our souls, we have to remove all self-centred or self-seeking tendencies which oppose his action. The foundation of our hope is God's goodness. We must believe in his love for us.

St. Thérèse describes holiness by saying that it 'does not consist in this or that practice, but lies in a disposition which renders us humble and little in God's hands, aware of our weakness and confident to the point of audacity in our Father's goodness.'

There is nothing to stop any soul from reaching the heights of divine love—so important for the Church as well as for itself—except its own self-sufficiency, its own independence, its own pride. Humility, we repeat, is the ladder to the summit of divine love. And self-renunciation, carried out in true simplicity, is the sure way of finding union with God. Poverty of spirit is the divinely announced title to the kingdom of heaven. Ultimately we must find God, we must renounce ourselves, we must be reduced to poverty, if not in this life, then in the next in the purifying fires of Purgatory. But now is the acceptable time, and St. Thérèse has been raised up to show us the true way.

We have already, in previous chapters, insisted upon the special propriety of humility in one who daily offers sacrifice to God; we feel bound to return to it. The Benedictine concept of humility as flowing from reverence to God is especially significant in this connection. A man who is called by his profession, as a priest is, to proclaim God's glory before heaven and earth, can find no better way of doing so continually than by true humility and spiritual childhood. St. Thérèse has given us one example. Another example, perhaps more akin to our own vocation, is that of Dom Marmion, the Dublin priest who became a Benedictine abbot and wrote what I think I may justly call the theology of spiritual childhood. Time and time again he insists in his writings that we must find all in Christ. Time and time again he urges us to lay down our will and judgement, our own way of seeing things, at the feet of Christ, and to tell him that we do not want anything except what comes from him, that we do not desire to do anything except what he, as the Word, from all eternity has decided for us; that in fact we should try to live in the spirit of St. Paul's words: 'Vivo autem, jam non ego: vivit vero in me Christus'[5] This of course means a high degree of self-abnegation. But that is not so difficult if only we can stir up a lively and unlimited faith in two things: in the burning personal love that God the Father has for each of us, a love which animates all his providential dispositions in our regard and which makes him ever solicitous for our welfare; and, secondly, in the infinite riches that are ours in Christ. His merits, infinite as they are, are *ours*. His claim upon the Father is *ours*. Truly has he borne all our infirmities and our weaknesses and has made ample provision for them. Truly has he taken away all our sins and has paid the price of our iniquities so that we may be delivered from them. In him there is nothing wanting to us in any grace.

If we have a real conviction of these two truths about God, we shall not be afraid to face the truth about ourselves. The ordinary priest who is not conscious of mortal sin finds it rather difficult to apply to himself what spiritual writers say about the nothingness and the sinfulness of the human creature. But there is a misunderstanding at the root of his outlook. He forgets that a man in the state of grace is neither a mere creature, nor is he alone. He is then a creature raised to a participation in the divine nature, and one in whose soul God dwells as a partner. To see the truth about ourselves we should abstract from the effect of grace, and view ourselves as we would be without it.

In this condition, in so far as the supernatural order is concerned, we are literally dead. We cannot make a single movement towards God, we have not even any claim upon God. All our riches are in Christ. In his name we can call upon God with the assurance that he must hear us. By his grace we can believe in God, we can hope in God, we can love God. By his strength we can live in God and for God. Gladly, then, let us glory in our infirmities that the power of Christ may dwell in us.

We have, therefore, to make up our minds whether we are going to live by our own strength or by the power of Christ. If we decide—as faced with a super-human vocation we must decide—that we must live by the power and strength of Christ, then immediately we are committed to that complete emptying of ourselves which is summed up in true humility and spiritual childhood.

[1] Aug. 14th 1921
[2] Matt. XVIII, 3
[3] Mark X, 15-16
[4] Oct. 8th 1938
[5] Gal. II, 20

CHAPTER THIRTEEN

RECITING THE DIVINE OFFICE

IT would be a mistake to make too sharp a distinction between the interior life of a priest and his external duties. All his priestly actions should flow from, and be animated by, his interior life. And his interior life can grow in depth and intensity through the proper performance of his priestly functions. In fact, any separation of the exterior work from the interior life is to be deplored; they are only two different aspects of the one same thing, the exterior work being but the expression of the interior life and love. This is especially true of the duty of reciting daily the diving office.

It is unfortunate that long prayers have become so associated in our minds with penance that we tend to look upon the recital of any vocal prayers of obligation merely as a penitential work, and to be concerned chiefly with the externals of its accomplishment. It is, of course, true that as far as the satisfaction of the particular obligation which is attached to the breviary is concerned, lip articulation is quite sufficient; and it is further true that, as far as fulfilment of the obligation is concerned, scruples must be ruthlessly avoided. But there is much more in the daily recitation of the office than a mere penance to be performed as a legal obligation under the penalty of serious sin. We priests tend to overlook, or at least to underestimate, the importance of one of the two aspects of our priesthood. As priests we stand between God and man. We speak to men and act on them in the name of God, but we also speak to God and worship him in the name of his people. It is this second aspect of our priestly vocation, an aspect which in many ways is its primary one, that we so often overlook. And even if we only consider the first-mentioned function—that of our duties to our flock—we still underestimate the importance of our breviary even in their regard. A priest seldom does so much for his flock as when he prays for them, and he seldom prays for them so effectively as when he recites the divine office.

Yet the primary importance of the divine office is its value as an act of divine worship. We know that when we as priests administer the sacraments, their principal effect is produced *ex opere operato*—independently of our personal merits and fervour. We know too that when we offer to God the sacrifice of the Mass, we offer him something which has a value in his eyes quite independent of our own unworthiness, for in our offering he sees Christ both offering and being offered. But we often forget, or at least fail to realize fully, how much there is in the divine office that has a value and an importance of its own. It is of course true that there is no question here of the *ex opere operato* manner of acting that belongs to the sacraments. But for all that, our position in the eyes of God when we are reciting the breviary is so official, so representative, so 'vicarious', that after the Mass and the sacraments there is hardly any other action which has a value—a great value—so independent of ourselves.

The very nature of the office itself suggests this.

The psalms and canticles which form the greater portion of it are the inspired work of the Holy Spirit. The rest is composed by the Church which has the aid of the Holy Spirit in all that concerns divine worship. So that in its content alone the breviary has a value— if one may so speak—in the eyes of God. To this there is added the fact that the priest reciting the breviary is not merely praying privately in his own name; he is an official representative of the whole Church speaking to God in her name and speaking with her claim to be heard. His own personal defects and de- merits do not affect his official status and importance. He comes before God as a representative of the Church which Christ loved and for which he delivered himself. The voice of the priest is the voice of the spouse, and has all the claim to be heard and the power to please that such a divinely redeemed spouse has. For this reason alone we priests should attach a very great importance to our recitation of the office, both as a means of satisfying God's claim to worship and praise, and also as a means of interceding with him for the needs of our people and of the whole Church.

But there is far more in it than that. For the Church is the Mystical Body of Christ, and when she speaks to the Father, Christ the Son of the Father is one with the Church, and he speaks too with her and in her. This is no mere metaphor. St. Augustine is most insistent on this union of Christ with the Church in the Church's prayer as is evident from the following quotations:

' We pray to him in the form of God; he prays in the form of the slave (i.e. ourselves). There he is the Creator; here he is in the creature. He changes not, but he takes the creature and changes it into himself, making us one man, head and body with himself. We pray therefore to him, and through him and in him; we pray with him and he prays with us; we recite this prayer of the psalms in him and he recites it in us.'[1]

'Let him rise up, this one chanter; let this Man sing from the heart of each of us, and let each of us be in this Man. When each one of you sings a verse, it is still this one Man that sings, since you are all one in Christ.'[2]

'You should of course consider that each of you is speaking but that primarily this one Man is speaking who reaches to the ends of the earth.'[3]

This is the great importance of the office: it is the prayer of Christ said by Christ to the Father of Christ, and when we recite the office, we enter into Christ, we put on Christ, we are one with Christ. In each of us the Father sees and hears Christ, his well-beloved Son in whom he is well pleased.

This view of the divine office will do much to correct the many mistakes we make in our attitude to it. First of all, we frequently complain that we find more devotion in other prayers and that the divine office does not arouse our fervour. No priest needs to be reminded that feelings of devotion are secondary and that their absence does not lessen the value of our prayer; such a 'dry' prayer, in fact, may be most valuable. But that is not really the point. It is not so much a question of replacing dryness by devotion or coldness by fervour. It is a question of replacing ourselves, of getting rid of ourselves, and of substituting for ourselves the person and the prayer of Christ.

Here we may note the importance of true humility which has occupied us so much in previous chapters. The truly humble man is never surprised at his own failure in prayer, nor does he presume to pray in his own name. Knowing what he is, and remembering what God is, he recognizes immediately his own complete inadequacy to pray to God as he should be prayed to, and he instinctively abandons himself and goes in search of Christ, who alone can pray to God and praise him adequately. And the man of faith and humility knows with complete certainty that Christ is only too willing to be found and to co-operate in such prayer and praise. Did he not tell us himself that he must be about his Father's business? And the man of faith, thus led by humility to seek Christ, takes up the breviary and, opening it, calls on God to come to his aid and then, united to Christ, allows him to use the lips of his creature to pray to the Father and to praise him in the name of his Son. If we but knew the gift of God! If we could only realize how completely Christ supplies for all our deficiencies when we say the office united to him by faith! The role of faith here is of essential importance. The just man lives by faith and it is by faith that Christ lives in our hearts. Faith must animate and rule our use of the breviary. It requires faith to realize all that the breviary should mean in a priest's life.

For in actual fact there is but one Priest, Christ himself, and we are only participators in his priesthood. And there is one great prayer of that Priest who, as the Word of God, is the only adequate praise of God; and, after the Mass, we have no more effective way of making that prayer and that praise our own than by reciting the divine office.

But it is important that we do not make the mistake of expecting to find a personal application for all the words of that office. Their full application is to be found in some member of that Mystical Body of Christ in whose name we are praying. We praise God on behalf of all creation; we thank him, we beg his grace and mercy, not merely for ourselves, but for all mankind. Many of the texts that the Church puts on our lips could refer to some soul under persecution, being tortured for his faith. Many texts, too, find their full application in the case of sinners who, having lost the grace of God, cannot come back to him unless he gives them grace. This, in fact, is a most important aspect of our official prayer as priests. There is no soul so helpless as the soul in mortal sin. No temporal privation or need, however urgent, can constitute such a claim on our charity as the supernatural needs of the soul in sin. It was particularly for such souls that our Lord came on earth and suffered and died. We must try to partake of his compassion for such souls. And apart from the Mass, there is no more effective way of helping these souls than by the recitation of the divine office. It is unfortunate that this apostolic aspect of the divine office is so often overlooked. It is true that many priests do realize that prayer is their primary task in the work of converting souls, though the realization is by no means so widespread or so complete as it should be. But even when the need of prayer in the apostolate is duly recognized, the supremacy of the divine office is overlooked and we have recourse to other prayer, personal prayer, much more dependent on our own dispositions than the official prayer which we say in the name of the Mystical Body of Christ. It is true that such personal prayers have their place and their importance; but they should not be allowed to supplant the divine office in our estimation or in our choice. There is no prayer more effiacious in drawing down the graces we need for our own souls or for those in whom we are interested.

We have mentioned the need for faith, and we should like to emphasize it, for its importance is not confined to the divine office. Sooner or later, all real progress in the spiritual life leads to a state where one must live and walk and work by faith. God hides himself and we can only believe in him. He hides his grace from us and even his readiness to grant it to us, and we must believe in his goodness and mercy. He hides from us the fruits of our labours in his vineyard, and yet we must continue to work by faith. It is true most priests have experienced obvious answers to prayer; but the time comes sooner or later when our prayers seem to lose their efficacy. This is particularly true of the divine office. Its generality, its vagueness of application, its extensive reference, conspire to hide from us its value. The fruit of our recitation of the psalms may be found in some other vineyard far from the scene of our own labours and may remain quite unknown to us. In fact the whole of the spiritual life may come to share in this apparent futility. St. Francis de Sales uses the comparison of a musician who has become deaf and who has no means of knowing whether he pleases those for whom he plays. The comparison can often find an application in the case of a priest reciting his office. For the moment, it has no appeal for himself; it seems dry, difficult, hard to understand, and incapable of exciting any devotion. Yet the priest must *believe*. He has the authority of the Church to rely upon, and he should always remember the insistence with which our Lord instructed his apostles about the essential principle of fruitfulness in the apostolate, which is to abide in him. How can we better abide in him than by entering into his prayer and making it our own? And in that very same instruction of our Lord, we should find an explanation for the aridity and difficulty that the divine office often assumes; for did he not warn us that when we had begun to bring forth fruit by abiding in him, his Father, the good husbandman, would purge and prune us so that we might bring forth more fruit? We have to be careful that, when God thus begins to lead us on to better things and to a more fruitful apostolate, we do not oppose his good work by throwing ourselves into activities where at least some meagre fruit is apparent and where our natural energies find some satisfaction in their activity. It is this very tendency and satisfaction that God wishes to 'purge'. The apostolate is, in all its branches, a supernatural work. It must be done by supernatural means, and one of the primary supernatural means is prayer, especially the prayer of Christ which we make our own in the divine office.

To appreciate properly the significance of the divine office one must have faith, and that faith must include not merely the prayer of Christ but Christ himself. We know that the merits of Christ are infinite and that these merits are shared with his Mystical Body, the Church. When, then, we pray in the name of Christ, we have these infinite merits of Christ pleading in our favour and outweighing all human demerits which could lessen the appeal of our prayer or obstruct its efficacy. This confident trust in the merits of Christ is one of the most important dispositions which must be ours when we come to say the office. The acts of faith and of hope which are required must be deliberately produced as a prelude to our prayer. We should not forget the part played by our will in these acts and we must *decide* to believe in God, and *decide* to hope in God, because he is God.

When it comes to the actual recitation of the office, many practical problems arise. They vary so much from one man to another that it would be hopeless to attempt their solution here. There is of course the general difficulty of sustaining one's attention and avoiding distraction. St. Thomas' doctrine on attention at prayer is well known: we may attend to the saying of our prayer, we may attend to the words we say, or we may attend to him to whom they are said. The special nature of the office adds a further possibility, for we may also attend to the Person who is saying the office with us, the Person who is really saying the office.

This possibility should open a way for many priests to approach the breviary with renewed zeal and courage. Experience has taught most of us something of our own limitations and of the inadequacy of our own prayers. An increasing realization of the nature of God, of his infinite perfection and goodness, adds a further motive for us to seek competent aid in praying to him and praising him. True zeal for his glory makes us seek union with Christ, who alone can give his Father adequate glory. True zeal for souls makes us cleave to the divine Saviour who came on earth to save souls, and who alone can properly intercede with his Father on their behalf. Turning then in this spirit to the divine office, we find there by faith our divine Saviour to whom we can 'attend' while we are reciting the words dictated by his Holy Spirit or provided by his spouse. The very commencement of the office is an appeal for such help: 'Deus in adjutorium meum intende: Domine ad adjuvandum me festina.' If we make the petition with sincerity and humble confidence we have already gone far to say our office properly.

But even to go so far on our way implies a fair degree of the interior life. Too often the life of a priest is directed towards souls instead of towards God. For that reason, he overlooks the importance of his own interior life and tends to resent, or at least to neglect, exercises and prescriptions that seem to take up time and energy which could, apparently, be employed more profitably for souls. To do this is to forget the first commandment. God requires the first fruits and the best of the flock. His claim on our direct worship is a primary one, and this includes his claim on the time necessary for the recitation of the divine office in praise of his name and glory. His glory is his own, he will not and cannot give it to another. For that reason it is of capital importance that we priests give him due honour by direct worship. And even our work for souls must be primarily work for God and must be done in a spirit which recognizes our complete dependence on him. Such a spirit will inevitably prompt us to give first place even in our apostolic work to prayer for his grace and help. And if we obey that prompting, we shall run no risk of depriving him of the glory of his mercy.

First things must come first. He has a first claim on our direct service. All other service—even the service of souls—must have him not only for its final end, but also for its first principle. The divine office plays a great part in ensuring the preservation of this perspective, and we must convince and frequently remind ourselves of the importance of the divine office not only in the direct worship of God but also in the apostolic care of souls. We repeat that after the Mass a priest can hardly find a more efficient way of

serving God and saving souls than by the devout recitation of the divine office.

[1] St. Augustine, *In Ps.* 85
[2] *In Ps.* 122, 1
[3] *In Ps.* 142

CHAPTER FOURTEEN

WITH OUR LADY

Since every priest is, by his office, a minister of grace, he cannot neglect devotion to our Lady, who is the Mediatrix of all graces. That alone would constitute a close relationship between the priest and our Lady. But the connection between them has an even wider foundation. Christ himself, whose priesthood we share, became a priest in the womb of his Mother. And the exercise of Christ's priesthood is directed to incorporating every soul into his Mystical Body, and to nourishing and developing that Body. Pius X has made it quite clear that just as Mary is the Mother of Christ's natural body, so too she is the Mother of his Mystical Body. Every priest, then, who works for the building up of the Mystical Body of Christ, is *de facto* working in partnership with Mary as well as with Christ. In fact, it is in a certain sense true that every priest shares in Mary's mystical maternity of souls.

Our Lady's part in the Sacrifice of Calvary is, of course, still a matter for theological discussion. That she took a considerable part in it is quite certain. Since our principal function as priests is to offer that sacrifice sacramentally in the Mass, Mary has for us no small significance. In fact, to cut short a discussion which could be prolonged at great length, we may state quite bluntly that *no priest can do without Mary*. He must have her help—and she certainly should have his devotion.

But even though she is so important for his work for other souls, yet Mary's first importance is for his own soul. Her function is to form Christ in the souls of men. Since the priest must be another Christ, to whom then can he come with more assurance than to Mary? Our constant prayer to her should be that she would form Christ in us, and form us in Christ. This constant and confident recourse to Mary, in season and out of season, is the first element in sacerdotal devotion to Our Lady. Every ministerial work we do as priests is done to Christ: 'Amen, I say to you, you did it to me'.[1] And because Mary is the Mother of Christ, she must have her part in all we do. If we could only realize how eager Mary always is to do something for Christ in the souls to whom we minister, and if we could only understand the immense power she has in regard to grace, we would joyfully and confidently invoke her aid in every single work of our ministry—in the name of Christ. She in turn would develop that charity, which should be the characteristic virtue of the priesthood, until it resembled the charity which is a burning fire in her own immaculate heart.

But even in regard to our direct relationship with God himself, our Lady's importance is tremendous. The truth is that the only adequate love and worship which God can receive is the love and worship given to him by a Divine Person—by Christ himself. No one appreciates this better than our Lady. No human being is so zealous for God's glory or so eager to have him loved as he should be loved as is Mary. She knows that it is only by being united to Christ and being quickened by the Spirit of Christ that we can give God due honour and due love. She is the divinely chosen means used by the Holy Ghost in bringing forth Christ on earth. If we go to her in the name of God—for his honour and for his love—asking her to give us her Son so that we may love God and serve him as Christ wishes to love and serve him in and through us, she will undoubtedly hear our prayer and give us Christ himself unless we set up obstacles by our own self-love and self-will.

Prayer, then, is the first work of devotion to our Lady. What particular form this prayer takes is not so important. The Rosary, however, put before us by Canon Law and urged upon us by so many Papal documents, is an obvious choice and should, of course, be recited daily by every priest. But we would suggest adding to it some more personal and intimate prayer—a prayer made in our own words and in our own way—in order that we may develop intimacy and union with our Lady. Such a prayer, of course, need not be too long, but it cannot be too fervent. Some form of a daily 'visit' to our Lady should be a feature of our programme. It should be the intimate meeting of a son with his mother, in which sincere candour and loving confidence predominate. The less formal 'prayers' one says on such occasions the better. But the fundamental bond ought to be that love and interest in Christ which we should have in common with our Lady. The principle must never be forgotten that the foundation, the motive, the purpose and the mainspring of devotion to Mary is devotion to Christ. We may confidently assert that no one has ever practised true devotion to Mary without thereby gaining a great increase in devotion to Christ.

Prayer, however, is not enough. Devotion to our Lady should lead us to imitate her example and to

follow her ideals. We can find a perfect summing-up
of her mind and doctrine in the only recorded words
she spoke to men: 'Whatsoever he shall say to you, do
ye.'[2] Obedience and abandonment to the will of God
in all its manifestations are the keynotes of Mary's life.
Her *Fiat* at the Annunciation is only the summing-up
of the entire consecration of herself to God and to his
will which animated every moment of her life.

It is, perhaps, possible to find in this lesson of precept
and example a deeper significance. Our Lady's function
is to incorporate us completely in Christ. Now this
requires our co-operation. Once we have received the
supernatural life of grace through the sacraments, the
completeness of our incorporation in Christ depends
on the degree of our submission to the will of God.
Unlike the members of a human body, the members of
the Mystical Body of Christ are masters of their own
actions. In every action, we can decide to do our own
will, and thus, despite the fundamental bond of incorporation into Christ, we for the moment live our own
life, quite separate from the life Christ lives in his
Mystical Body. In so far as we remove our actions
from the influence of the Holy Ghost, who resembles
the soul in the Mystical Body of Christ, we separate
ourselves from Christ. Whereas when the Holy Ghost
has complete control over all our actions, when, in
fact, we are completely led by the will of God, we are
living our full mystical life in Christ, no matter how
prosaic or commonplace our actions may be—so long
as they are the will of God. Christ came on earth to
do the will of the Father, and wherever the will of the
Father is being done, there Christ is doing it in partnership with the created agent. Mary's exhortation to
obedience thus lays down the principle of co-operation

in the maternity of the Mystical Body. Christ himself told us that he who does the will of his Father in heaven is his mother.[3] By devoting ourselves to doing the will of God and accepting all its manifestations we are not merely imitating Mary, but we are co-operating in her work as mother of the Mystical Body of Christ in our own souls. It is extraordinary how true devotion to Mary always leads to devotion to Christ, to the Holy Spirit and finally to the Blessed Trinity.

But there are other outstanding virtues which characterized our Lady's life and which call for our imitation. Her humility is one of her greatest glories. Her virginity made her body holy, but her humility gave her holiness of spirit. By her virginity she pleased God, but by her humility she drew God down to this earth. The whole Incarnation is characterized by humility. And it was by her humility that our Lady most closely corresponded to the dispositions of her Son in his Incarnation. Being his Mother, she had to resemble what he was to be. To be humble, one must accept the truth, especially the truth about oneself; one must adapt oneself willingly to things as they are; one must will what God has willed in the way which he has willed it. Our Lady ignored herself completely. She looked always to God, never worrying or even asking what effect she produced on others. She never compared or preferred herself to others. She avoided all singularity, all wish for distinction; she always showed candour, simplicity and perfect rectitude of intention. But if one may try to sum up her humility in a phrase, it is not enough to say that hers was a humility which ignored itself, or which kept silent, or which effaced itself; one must go further and describe it as the humility which completely forgets itself. There is ample field here in this matter for every priest to try to imitate Mary's humility. It will be a life-long work, it will only be achieved completely by special graces, but it is what Mary, and not only Mary but Christ himself, has taught us in every moment of their lives.

There are, however, many degrees of devotion to our Lady. If we are asked to suggest some means of growing in this devotion we would put forward the following. First, we must study our Lady, and our own vocation in reference to our Lady. Secondly, we must continually pray for devotion to our Lady, begging especially the gift of a filial piety to her. Thirdly, we should endeavour to imitate her favourite virtues: in particular her charity, her humility, her simplicity, her spirit cf faith and of prayer, her careful custody of her heart; but above all one must imitate her in her complete devotion to Jesus and to his interests. Fourthly, we should second her in her apostolate, acting as her junior partner, so to speak, working in dependence and reliance upon her who is so intimately connected with the work of our salvation. Fifthly, if one wishes to go further, there is the complete consecration of oneself to Mary. This is not a way which appeals to every one. It is, however, a short cut to sanctity. Associated with the name of St. Louis Grignon de Montfort who expounded the doctrine in his book *True Devotion to Our Lady*, it acquired a special significance when he was canonized. This consecration to our Lady consists in making over to her as completely as we can all that we have, all that we do, all that we are, all that we acquire, past, present, and future—in a word, in giving to her everything of which we have any power to dispose. We give Mary our body that it may be used in her service in activity or in suffering as she desires. We consequently accept all the dispositions of Providence in regard to health, strength, sickness, life or death, for the whole of our days on earth. We give Mary the right to dispose of us and of all our material possessions, relying on her maternal care to provide for us. But still more, we place all our faculties at Mary's disposal for the service of her Son. We employ them for her and not for ourselves, and we commit the outcome of all our actions to her protection, accepting failure or success with prudent indifference. Our soul itself we give to her, with the Christ-life that Baptism has planted within us, relying on her to ensure its sanctification, its perseverance, its salvation and its ultimate union with God in heaven.

We go even further. All our prayers, and all the prayers that are said for us, even after death, are made over to her to apply according to her own intentions. The supernatural value of our works is included in our offering so that she can use their satisfactory and impetratory effect as she pleases; even our merits, in so far as they can be transferred, belong to her. We make no reserve; all that is in any way ours is hers to draw on and to use as she pleases. It is of capital importance to realize that all this consecration to our Lady is only a means—but to our mind *the* most efficacious means— to an end. The end of it all is that we may belong more securely and more completely to her Son Jesus Christ. He asked us to 'abide' in him. It is in order that we may abide in him that we give ourselves to Mary. We shall get some idea of the underlying purpose if we recall how our Lord's Body was formed on earth. Until he was born every particle of his sacred Flesh and Blood was drawn from Mary. By taking the products of the earth in food and drink, Mary made them part of herself and thus they became part of our Lord. Even after the Nativity this process continued, for in the beginning he was nourished by our Lady herself, and then by the work of her hands when she prepared his food. Now there is an analogous pattern in the formation of the Mystical Body of Christ, for this Body is formed by the mediation of Mary. The more, therefore, we give ourself to Mary, the more certainly and the more completely are we given by her to Christ.

It must be remembered that this devotion is no passing act; it is a life-long policy, an habitual attitude of mind, a continued turning of the heart. It needs frequent renewal, but often a smile or a glance towards our Lady is all that is necessary. It is not a devotion to be adopted without deliberation and reflection. Those who wish to find a more detailed account of it should read the two small works of St. Louis Grignon de Montfort. Tanquercy sums up the devotion in each of his two books, *The Spiritual Life* and *Doctrine and Devotion*. Once this offering has been made, we should be docile to all Mary's directions, and in the matter of our own spiritual advance, we should let her form us in sanctity and guide our apostolate. In everything, spiritual and temporal, we should live in confident dependence on Mary's care, seeing in everything that happens her arrangement.

If our devotion to her is sincere and generous, we shall be amazed at her solicitude for us. First of all, we shall find an extraordinary peace in our own souls. We are in Mary's hands, and she can and will look after us much better than we can ourselves. Then our work is under her protection and guidance. No matter what help we need, no matter what special grace is required to achieve God's purpose, we are sure that Mary's all-powerful intercession will obtain it. Every priest knows the numerous little things—meetings, books, words, ideas—resulting apparently from chance, which play so great a part in the apostolate. Once we have put Mary in charge of our lives, these things begin to multiply in an amazing manner, so that Mary's intervention is almost palpable. The more generous we are with Mary, the more munificent she will be with us.

No one need think that such devotion to our Lady will interfere with our direct approach to Jesus Christ. Quite the contrary. Union with our Lady gives us a new confidence and assurance in approaching our Lord. Our sins no longer lessen our spontaneity of approach, for our consciousness of Mary's support removes our diffidence. And this approach to Christ in union with our Lady prepares us for the still more important approach with Christ to God. She thus trains us in the essential lesson of Christianity. In fact we can even go to our Lady in the name of Christ, reminding her that what she does for us is done for Christ so that we are giving her new opportunities of doing something for her beloved Son. We can even plead our defects and our demerits in our favour, by reminding her that she never had to overcome repugnance in loving and serving Jesus in himself, whereas in loving and serving him in us who are sinners, she can show her love for him in a new way. Or we can approach Christ directly and offer him an opportunity of showing his love for his mother, because, since we are completely hers, anything he does for us is ultimately done for her.

The consciousness that Mary can apply the fruits of our work can give us a new assurance in our apostolate. With the best will in the world we can never of ourselves know where our forces can be best employed for the glory of God. Even within the limits laid down by obedience, there is always room for individual choice of effort and emphasis. If all is given to Mary, we know that she will apply the results of our efforts just exactly at the particular point where they are most needed. Here let us remind the reader that there is a double effect of the actions of our apostolate. One is the immediate and what we might somewhat inaccurately call the 'natural' effect of our efforts. For example, the effect of a sermon should be some result in the minds and hearts of our hearers. But there is another effect, a deeper and more supernatural one. If it is our duty to preach, then it is God's will, and we can approach our sermon as an act of loving submission to God, animated by love for him, preaching just because he wants us to preach. By this act we 'abide' in him; and by abiding in him, we bring forth fruit. This fruit may be brought forth anywhere in the Church, and it is, in some ways, a much more important result than the one immediately produced on our present congregation. A priest's life could be a fruitless failure where his immediate flock is concerned—as sometimes happens, more or less, in the mission fields —and yet be productive of great fruit at some other place and perhaps some other time in the Church. The death of Christ was the most fruitful moment of his life on earth. So too our apparent failures may be our most fruitful works, especially if we are in the hands of Mary.

Much more could be said on the part played by devotion to Mary in the life of the priest. Her charity and our imitation of it call for further discussion. Meanwhile let it suffice to quote the words of Pius X: 'There is no more certain or efficacious way of uniting all to Christ than by Mary . . . . Clearly, there is no other alternative for us than to receive Christ from the hands of Mary.'[4] We must, then, be sure to give her her proper place in our lives.

[1] Matt. XXV, 40
[2] John II, 5
[3] Cf. Matt. XII, 50
[4] *Ad diem illum*

CHAPTER FIFTEEN

THE TEACHING OF ST. PIUS X

THE canonisation of Pope Pius X drew special attention to his teaching on the spiritual life of the priest. Not only did he write with the authority of the vicar of Christ, but it may be truly said that he taught nothing which he himself did not practise. An outline, then, of his spiritual teaching should be very much to our present purpose in these pages.

After his elevation to the Papacy, St. Pius soon announced to the world what he intended to do. His purpose he declared to be that expressed in the words of St. Paul: ' Instaurare omnia in Christo ut videlicet sit omnia, et in omnibus Christus '[1]: that is to re-establish all things in Christ, so that Christ might be all and in all. With this inspired purpose in mind, he appeals to the Episcopate to assist him by their personal holiness, their wisdom, their actions, striving to give God the glory due to him and having no other purpose than to form Christ in all souls. As a first step to this end he appeals to the bishops to spare no effort that Christ be formed in those priests who are destined for the work of forming him in others. And the words of the Holy Father are of tremendous significance for us priests: 'How can they fulfil this function unless they themselves have first of all put on Christ—and that in such a way that they can say with St. Paul: "I live, now not I; but Christ liveth in me . . . To me, to live is Christ".[2] ' The general vocation to be filled with the fullness of Christ has a special application to the priest; for he must be another Christ, not merely by showing the power of Christ, but by imitating his deeds so that he may be his living image. This is a high ideal, but it is the ideal which must be that of every true priest. And the Holy Father, pursuing his purpose of re-establishing all things in Christ, goes on to discuss the formation of priests upon whom the whole work depends.

Reminding the priest of his obligation to teach and to bear fruit, St. Pius reminds him that in all his work nothing is more effective than charity. It is a fallacy to hope to lead souls to God by bitter zeal. It is true, the Pope says, that St. Paul exhorts St. Timothy to 'reprove, entreat, rebuke', but he adds 'in all patience'.[3] Indeed we would draw attention to a further addition, for the full text reads 'in all patience and doctrine.' The Pope puts before us the example of Christ himself who could say: 'Come to me all you that labour and are burdened, and I will refresh you'[4] and in those who labour and are burdened he sees a reference to those in sin and in error. Christ's wonderful meekness, mildness, sympathy and kindness should be an example for us priests. And there follows in the original Encyclical (E Supremi, October 4th, 1903) a moving appeal for charity in all the works of the apostolate. The prophet Isaias is quoted as giving us a portrait of the heart of Christ in the words: 'He shall not cry out nor have respect to person . . . the bruised reed he shall not break and smoking flax he shall not quench.'[5] Our charity must be patient and kind, even to those who are our opponents or our enemies. Like St. Paul we must bless when we are reviled, we must be patient when we are persecuted, we must pray when we are blasphemed. For, as the holy heart of the Pope inspires him to say, 'they are not as evil as they seem to be.' They may have been led astray by bad habits, or the example and the advice of others; their own prejudices and shame may have driven them to the wrong side; but their wills are not as evil as their behaviour might indicate. To the darkness of their souls the flame of charity can bring light and peace; and although it may take time to bear fruit, charity is never fatigued, never gives up. In any case, God has promised his rewards not for the fruit of our labours but for the good will that animates them.

The Holy Father, then, is insistent on the lesson taught us by the Good Shepherd: 'Learn of me, because I am meek, and humble of heart.'[6] St. Pius himself was a model of meekness, and the mildness of saintly men in dealing with sinners is a commonplace in Christian history. The saints, and above all our Divine Saviour, are our safest guides. We shall do well to model our ministry on his and theirs. 'This man receiveth sinners': that was the impression made by our Lord on the Jews of his day. His methods and those of his saints are the best and will do far more good in the long run than anything approaching harshness. We must, indeed, 'reprove, entreat and rebuke' when occasion demands, but even when we do so, if our people see in us something of the gentleness and kindness of the Sacred Heart, they will listen much more readily to our warnings. The priest, like Christ, must be zealous for the honour of his Father's house; but, again like Christ, he must also be 'the friend of publicans and sinners.'

So urgent did Pius X consider the sanctification of

the clergy that he returned to the subject in a special instruction, *Haerenti Animo*.[7] He reminds us that our priesthood is given us not merely for ourselves but also for others. Priests are the light of the world and the salt of the earth. We must preach not only by word but by example. Without holiness we are as useless as the savourless salt. To the question of this need and obligation of holiness in the priest, St. Pius frequently returns. He assumes the obligation and discusses the way it can be fulfilled in the Letter approving the Pia Unio *Cum nobis*.[8] In his Letter to the Clergy, *Haerenti Animo*, he is more explicit. We exercise our priestly functions not in our own name, but in the name of Christ. And we are called by Christ to this work not as his servants but as his friends. True friendship results from a unity of wills: 'Idem velle, idem nolle, ea demum firma amicitia est.' We must therefore have the mind of Christ, and share in his dispositions, his outlook, his purpose. In fact we must go further, and here St. Pius sums up in a phrase the whole spiritual life of the priest: 'Est igitur nobis persona Christi gerenda.' We have to reproduce Christ in ourselves and in our lives. This is our vocation and this is our purpose.

Christ's own dispositions, Christ's own purpose, Christ's own mind, are most perfectly expressed and summed up in his Sacrifice. We have to renew this Sacrifice every time we offer Mass and, as Pius tells us, we must try to conform our minds to his as he offered himself as an unspotted victim to God. If the former sacrifices of the Old Law, which were merely shadows of what was to come, demanded so much holiness in those who offered them, what obligations are ours, whose victim is Christ himself? Nothing short of a complete dedication of our whole being to God can correspond to the sacrifice we offer.

The standard St. Pius sets for us is high. He expects as great a difference between the life of a good Christian and that of a priest as between heaven and earth. But we must form a correct view of what is required of us: and here St. Pius corrects an error that is not unknown even in our own times. 'Some', he writes, 'feel that a priest's perfection is to be found in his spending himself completely in the service of others; they would not have him worry too much about those virtues which are sometimes called "passive"; all his energy and purpose should be concentrated on the "active" virtues.' This view the Holy Pontiff brands as absolutely fallacious, and makes his own the teaching of his predecessor, Leo XIII: 'Christ is the Master and Exemplar of all holiness, all true holiness must be modelled on him.' Nothing has changed the example he gave us of meekness, humility of heart and obedience even unto death. Self-abnegation is still the foundation of sanctity, and is the source of much of a priest's fruitfulness. To be swayed by ambition, by honours, by success, by pleasure, is to depart from the rule laid down by our Lord: 'If any man will come after me, let him deny himself.'[9]

The Pope, of course, does not mean that we can neglect the duties of our ministry. We have been hired by the Master to work in the vineyard. We must be about our Father's business. But we must remember that, especially in the ministry, we are nothing of ourselves. We have been chosen as God's instruments but not because of our merits. For St. Paul reminds us: 'The foolish things of the world hath God chosen, that he may confound the wise; and the weak things of the world hath God chosen that he may confound the strong; and the base things of the world, and things that are contemptible hath God chosen, and the things that are not, that he might bring to nought the things that are.'[10] Having quoted this text, Pius proceeds to lay down doctrine of capital importance for every priest. Here we render rather freely: 'There is only one thing which unites man to God, only one thing which makes him pleasing to God and keeps him from being an unworthy minister of his mercy, and that is holiness of life and of manners. If this—which is the super-eminent knowledge of Jesus Christ—is lacking in the priest, everything is lacking. For without this holiness, even that extensive knowledge of doctrine (which we are trying to promote in the clergy), even the greatest dexterity and skill in dealing with souls, while it may produce some good for the Church or for particular souls, quite often is a deplorable cause of harm . . . Holiness, and holiness only, makes us what our divine vocation requires us to be, men walking in newness of life who, as St. Paul exhorts us,[11] show ourselves to be ministers of God in labours, in watchings, in fastings, in chastity, in knowledge, in long-suffering, in sweetness, in the Holy Ghost, in charity unfeigned,—men whose whole tendency is to heavenly things and who strive in every way to lead others to God.'

The Holy Father then proceeds to point out that the first essential step to acquire this holiness is to pray and to pray earnestly. So close is the connection between holiness and the practice of prayer that the former cannot exist without the latter. Our Lord's own example preaches this doctrine eloquently. He spent whole nights in prayer. He frequently prayed in the Temple and even in the agonies of death he prayed with a loud cry and with tears to the Father. 'This then we can hold as certain and unquestionable', says St. Pius, 'that a priest, in order to be what his office demands, must be devoted (*eximie deditum*) to the practice of prayer.' To this prayer must be added the practice of reflection and meditation. 'No priest can neglect this without grave carelessness and considerable harm to his own soul.' It is an essential foundation for the sustaining of our supernatural outlook and purpose. And a priest must develop a facility in remembering and in striving after heavenly things, for he must frequently speak and treat of the next world. He must then so arrange his life above all merely human things, that whatever he does in his sacred ministry he should do according to God, inspired and guided by faith. This necessary habit of mind and almost natural partnership with God depends greatly on daily meditation. Those who neglect this daily exercise show a sad example of its importance. For they have lost that *sensus Christi*, and are wrapped up in terrestrial affairs, performing their sacred functions carelessly, coldly and perhaps unworthily. And the Holy Father speaks of the deadly blindness of those who are so foolish as to think that time given to prayer and meditation is time wasted. Such neglect and contempt of prayer leads to pride and contumaciousness and to very many other troubles which St. Pius prefers not to mention. He then discusses the need for regular spiritual reading, for proper examination of conscience, and for general fervour in prayer and the practice of virtue. And again he repeats the fundamental principle—that the motive for all our efforts is the example of Christ. 'For if the priest is called another Christ, and is indeed so by communication in Christ's power, is it not essential that he should also be called another Christ, and be so in fact by imitating the deeds of Christ? Therefore let our principal preoccupation be the consideration of the life of Jesus Christ.'

Texts from the writings of St. Pius could be multiplied but there is no need to quote more. His life itself was a sermon. He only preached what he himself practised. For him, to be a priest was to be a victim, to be at everyone's disposal. He once said that 'to be a priest is to be bound to fatigue—the two are synonymous.'

If we may return to something of which we have spoken already: his insistence on charity is of great practical importance. Two places there are in which a priest's charity should never fail him. One is the pulpit and the other is the confessional. It is true, of course, that in the pulpit abuses must sometimes be denounced and shortcomings criticized. But there is always the danger that such criticism should come to occupy a disproportionate place in our preaching. We are sent primarily to preach the Gospel, the word of God. Only in a secondary way are we called upon to speak of the failings of men. Any inversion of that order can only do more harm than good. If our preaching is positive, if Sunday after Sunday we speak to our people of the great central truths of Christianity, that will give them a basis for leading a full Christian life. And it will achieve far more than anything else. And even when we have to criticize, we can do it in a Christlike way, in a way which makes it clear that we love the sinner while we hate the sin. 'If you want to draw love out, you must pour love in.' So spoke St. John of the Cross, and it might not be the worst of mottoes for the priest in the pulpit.

There is no need to emphasize to any priest how important it is always to be kind in the confessional.

Nor is there any need to tell him that it is sometimes difficult. Here, as always, Christ is our model. His gentleness was never more apparent than with the repentant sinner; and in the welcome of the father to the prodigal son, we can catch some glimpse of what Christ wants us to be when we take his place in the confessional. It may not be easy but it will be abundantly fruitful.

But all that, like everything else worth while in a priest's life, is impossible, unless we are living an interior life of union with Christ. Prayer, reflection and reading are essential foundations. No priest dare neglect them. He who does, even on the plea of devoting more time to the apostolate, is fooling himself and separating himself from God. St. Pius has warned us and has shown us the way.

[1] Cf. Ephes. I, 10 and Col. III. 11
[2] Gal. II, 20; Philipp. I, 21
[3] 2 Tim. IV, 2
[4] Matt. XI, 28
[5] Isaias XLII, 2
[6] Matt. XI, 29
[7] Aug. 4th 1908
[8] Dec. 28th 1903
[9] Matt. XVI, 24
[10] 1 Cor. I, 27-28
[11] 2 Cor. VI, 5 et seq.

CHAPTER SIXTEEN

CHARITY, A PRIESTLY VIRTUE

IF there is any one virtue which must be especially characteristic of the priest, it is the virtue of charity. This is true not merely because charity is the queen of virtues and the bond of perfection, but also because of the very nature of the priesthood. A priest is ordained, for *others*. He is dedicated to God and to souls. He *is* no longer his own; he belongs first to God and then to souls, especially those souls committed to his care. He is the shepherd who, not being a mere hireling, must lay down his life for his flock if that be necessary. He may not be asked to lay down his life literally for his sheep, but he *is* asked to lay it down by *living* for them. To repeat that rather inelegant summary, a priest must not merely 'deliver the goods', for he is another Christ and Christ delivered himself.

This vocation to deliver himself gives us some measure of the degree of charity required in the priest. Charity, of course, is a single virtue; by it we love God, and by the same virtue we love our neighbour. And St. John is quite drastic in his censure of those who claim that they can love God without loving their neighbour. The love of God is, of course, fundamental, but if it is sincere it must lead to a love for souls, and it is of this fraternal charity in the priest that we wish

to speak here. And it is so important that we must
commence by letting the Holy Spirit himself speak of
it through St. Paul, in words that are so well known as
to be easily overlooked. 'Charity is patient, is kind:
charity envieth not, dealeth not perversely, is not
puffed up, is not ambitious, seeketh not her own, is not
provoked to anger, thinketh no evil: rejoiceth not in
iniquity, but rejoiceth with the truth: beareth all things,
believeth all things, hopeth all things, endureth all things.
Charity never falleth away.'[1] No priest can doubt that
these words have a very special meaning for him; it is
enough to recall the words that are spoken to him on
the morning of his ordination: 'Ministros Ecclesiae suae
fide et opere debere esse perfectos, seu geminae dilec-
tionis, Dei scilicet et proximi, virtute fundatos.' And
again: 'Accipe vestem sacerdotalem, per quam caritas
intelligitur; potens enim Deus ut augeat tibi caritatem
et opus perfectum.' These words exhort the priest to
the perfection of charity towards his neighbour as well
as towards God, and they promise him that God is
powerful enough to overcome his human limitations
and weakness and to bring him to the perfection which
he requires. With this assurance we need not be afraid
to examine what should be our charity as priests.

Charity, of course, has its foundation in the interior,
but perhaps it is better to begin by considering its
exterior manifestation in speech. And it is hardly an
unfair test to estimate a priest's charity by his speech
with and about his fellow-priests. How do we stand
up to this test? That is a question which each of us
must answer for himself, but it may be a guide to set
the question in its context of the standard of charity in
speech among our people. And in this matter an outside and somewhat critical view may be worth re-

peating. More than one visitor to Ireland, while paying tribute to the superlative qualities of Irish Catholicism, has been disappointed at the way Irish Catholics speak of one another. This, no doubt, is in relation to what they expect in a fully Catholic country, but at any rate the picture as they see and depict it is hardly flattering. A tendency to speak ill of our neighbour and to regard it as harmless because what we say is true, a readiness to indulge in gossip which sometimes borders on serious calumny—these things appear to our critics as strangely out of tune with the vigorous Catholic life of our country.

It is not a complimentary picture and it may be a highly exaggerated one. Visitors may fail to get the 'feel' of a place and may see things out of all proportion. It would be imprudent unreservedly to accept such a verdict, but it might be equally imprudent to dismiss it as entirely baseless. No one is in a better position than the secular priest to pass judgement on the facts, and if our national standards in this matter are too low, he alone can do something about it.

But there is a further consideration. If our standards are too low, if the atmosphere is wrong, there is at least the danger that even we priests may ourselves have become infected. And this could mean that quite unconsciously we may have come to adopt too low a standard in the way we speak to and about our fellow-priests. There is a special danger in the field of wit and humour. The amusing remark can sometimes be caustic and the sally of wit may easily carry a barb. It is hard to lay down practical rules in this matter; the formal speech of the continent would be quite an affectation in an Irish presbytery and the absence of humour would make conversation unbearable. But there is a big difference between laughing *at* someone and laughing *with* someone. Christian charity will try rather to laugh *with* one's neighbour than *at* him, and Christian perfection, even when not of a high degree, will refrain completely from laughing at him. If that standard appears too high, we can only say that our Lord insisted that what we do to our brother is done to him. To mock a fellow-priest is to mock at Christ, and no *eutrapelia* can justify that! Further, we might point out that humour of the dangerous kind often springs from motives that are far from Christian. To 'take the other fellow down a peg', to enhance one's own superiority, are not the promptings of Christian charity. We have it on the authority of the Holy Ghost that 'if any man offend not in word, the same is a perfect man.'[2] Our speech with our neighbour, especially with our fellow-priests, is therefore a subject on which even the best of us would do well to examine ourselves.

But whatever about our speech, there is no doubt that a generous charity animates all our other relations with our fellow-priests. Charity, however, must extend beyond our fellow-priests; it has a special reference to our parishioners. Here, perhaps, we may find ourselves at fault. The demands of charity go much beyond the demands of justice, and we may be tempted sometimes to limit the service of our parishioners to what justice demands. To discuss details would be tedious and perhaps invidious, but one question at least which we might all put ourselves is this: Am I as approachable as I should be? The humblest or most sinful member of our flock should feel that he can come readily to us in his troubles or his needs, should feel quite sure of his welcome. If, through our fault, he feels otherwise, it is nothing short of a tragedy. Admittedly every priest must surround himself at times with a certain reserve. He has to find time for his prayers, his studies, and to provide for many other calls on his services. But he is also a disciple of a Master of whom it was stated as a characteristic trait: 'This man receiveth sinners.' Is the same thing characteristic of us? It should really be so, for we also must be good shepherds. If our Divine Master's example impels us to seek out the lost sheep in kindness, how much more readily should we receive the same lost sheep when he seeks us out himself? To put it in a word, we must be Christlike, and the sinner was never afraid to approach our Saviour.

True fraternal charity goes, of course, far beyond the corporal works of mercy. There is—at least there should be—a certain supernatural 'solidarity' between the priest and those allotted to his care. They should always have a prominent place in his prayers. But if we are going to imitate our Lord fully we should go further. We might even take their sins on our own shoulders, at least to the extent of offering the sacrifice of the Mass to atone for them. There is here wide scope for charity and for imitation of our Saviour— who is the Saviour of his Body, who delivered himself for us, and who sanctified himself for us. We priests have to go and do likewise.

To attempt to enumerate the various ways of practising fraternal charity, or to catalogue the offences against it to which we are liable would serve little useful purpose. Far more important it is to probe the underlying causes of our failure. Failure in charity can generally be traced to two sources: lack of a true interior life and lack of humility. The truly humble man is not touchy or aggressive. Wounded vanity does not animate his remarks and his wit is free from self-seeking. His zeal has no bitterness and his corrections are marked by benignity. Knowing his own need of God and conscious of his lowly position in God's sight, he gladly and cheerfully sees and seeks God in his neighbour. The ministry to him is not an exercise of power but of service. All this, however, is possible only where there is a true interior life.

This is really the root of the whole problem. It might, perhaps, be possible to build up all the externals of the active apostolate, with a minimum of interior charity, but unless that charity animates all else, 'it profiteth us nothing.' That, of course—if it were at all possible—would be an extreme case. Yet something of such an empty activity could develop in the life of a priest who neglects his interior life. It is possible to approach the work of the parish or the mission in a spirit somewhat akin to that in which a professional or business man approaches his daily duties. The organization of the parish or of the mission can be animated by the same natural zeal that inspires many secular undertakings. Even the work of saving souls can degenerate into something resembling the ideal of a teacher who merely sees his pupils as so many ciphers to be pushed through an examination. Typical of such teachers and such shepherds is concentration on the particular test envisaged, without paying much attention to how the results are achieved or what spirit animates the performances so crowned. Whatever may be said about such teaching, such preaching is certainly disastrous. It merely produces—or tries to produce—external results, generally of a negative type, while what God wants is our hearts and our love. The priest who justifies his existence by the fact that he 'puts the fear of God into his parishioners' is hardly the shepherd after God's own heart. Such zeal is often false zeal and does not flow from true divine charity.

The way to correct our failings in this matter and to advance in true charity is through familiar intercourse with our Saviour by reading, by reflection and by prayer. Indeed we should also find a place for our Lady in these meetings, for no one has so faithfully imitated the charity of the heart of Jesus as she has. It is impossible for us to be in frequent contact with Jesus or with his Mother and at the same time not to improve in fraternal charity. The gentleness of Jesus, his kindness, his thoughtfulness, his compassion for the unfortunate, his sympathy for sinners stand out from the story of his life and of his death. Sympathy with sinners is a form of charity that calls for a special place in our lives. It was this sympathetic compassion for the sinner that brought Jesus on earth and led him to his death on the Cross, and we who are 'other Christs' must share in this spirit of sympathy and compassion. It is noticeable that the holiest men are the most compassionate and benign in their dealings with sinners. Those of us who wish to join them in their imitation of Christ must seek it where they found it, in union with him. Of all men it is only Christ who could really claim that sin was an offence against himself; yet he is the most forgiving and compassionate of all. We sometimes would give the impression in our dealings with sinners that we ourselves, rather than God, are the persons offended. We have to learn of him who is meek and humble of heart and who suffered and died for those who offended him.

In the matter of fraternal charity we are too prone to overlook the significance of the doctrine of the Mystical Body of Christ. As Christians, we are no longer our own, we belong to the Body of Christ. As members of that Body we have to live according to the law of all such organic life, which is that each cell, each member, each organ, lives for the good of the whole body and not merely for itself. In any other organism the members are animated and ruled by whatever principle of life is common to the whole body. Each member, normally, has no individual choice. Willy-nilly, it submits. In the Mystical Body of Christ things are not the same. The spirit which gives the whole Body unity is the Spirit of Christ, the Holy Ghost. He takes possession of each of us in baptism when we are incorporated into the Body of Christ. But he does not destroy our freedom of choice. In each of our actions we have complete liberty—either to act under his leadership or to follow our own will. To the extent that we subject ourselves to him, we are the sons of God and living healthy members of the Body of Christ. Charity is poured forth in our hearts by this same Spirit, and unless we give that charity free play in our lives, we constrain the Spirit of God and resist his work in our souls.

Because, then, we are members of the Body of Christ, we must live not for ourselves but for the whole Body. This is true even of ordinary Christians, it is still more true of us who are priests. And because our fellow-men are members of the same Body, either actually or potentially, we must love and serve Christ in them. To resist the inspirations of fraternal charity is to offend Christ in our own souls, for it is he who wishes to serve his members through us, and also to neglect him in our neighbour, for it is he who wishes to be served in our neighbours. A spirit of faith and a deep appreciation of the nature of the Christian life are needed for a life

of true fraternal charity. But that is what our Lord
would have us achieve. One has only to read his last
address to his disciples to realize what our lives as
priests should be.

St. John the Evangelist was ordained a priest at the
last supper and he commences his record of this last
festival with the account of our Lord's washing the feet
of his disciples. He prefaces the account with the significant words: 'Jesus . . . having loved his own who
were in the world, he loved them unto the end'[3] and
he records our Lord's commentary at the end of this
touching ceremony: 'Know you what I have done to
you? You call me Master and Lord. And you say well:
for so I am. If I then being *your* Lord and Master,
have washed your feet, you also ought to wash one
another's feet. For I have given you an example, that
as I have done to you, so you do also.'[4] And soon we
read the record of the new commandment: 'A new
commandment I give unto you: That you love one
another as I have loved you, that you also love one
another. By this shall all men know that you are my
disciples, if you have love one for another.'[5] Our
Saviour then goes on to expound the mysterious unity
which makes us branches of the Vine which is himself,
and he adds: 'As the Father hath loved me, I also have
loved you. Abide in my love . . . This is my commandment, that you love one another, as I have
loved you.'[6]

Here we have our Lord's teaching for us priests.
He has given us an example; we are to do as he has
done to us. We are to love one another as he has loved
us. What has he done to us? How has he loved us?
The answer is found in the sacred mysteries we celebrate
every morning at the altar and which the Church, in

giving us the power to celebrate, enjoined on us to imitate. Christ became a victim for us and for all who sin against him. He expects us to do as he did. That is the measure of charity which Christ demands of his priests.

It is literally a tremendous obligation, and one which it would be utterly impossible to fulfil without his special grace. But the very sacrament which gives us his sacrifice to offer and to imitate also gives us himself and his Holy Spirit that we may find in him the strength to do as he does. For us priests the Mass is a well of doctrine, an unending source of light, a spring of strength and a centre for our whole life. We cannot ponder over its meaning and its mysteries too much. But we must approach its consideration in a spirit of good will, for we must be prepared to go and do like-wise. This will be possible only if we keep up all the exercises by which an interior life is sustained: reading, reflection and prayer. Without these our charity will grow cold. Human motives will replace it as the main-spring of our work, and without charity all that we do, all that we are, is nothing. It is of the utmost importance then that we devote ourselves to an interior life of union with our Lord, that we allow him to live his life in us and to serve himself in his members.

[1] 1 Cor. XIII, 4-8
[2] James III, 2
[3] John XIII, 1
[4] John XIII, 13-15
[5] John XIII, 34-35
[6] John XV, 9-12

CHAPTER SEVENTEEN

LIVING IN CHRIST

IF our lives as priests are not so holy as they should be, it is very often because the ideal which animates them is not sufficiently high. *Sacerdos, alter Christus*. That, perhaps, is the most pregnant expression of what our ideal should be. The *character* impressed on our souls in ordination makes us 'other Christs', participators in the priesthood of Christ. And if we are to be true to our vocation, our minds and hearts must be filled with the spirit which was his.

What was the spirit of our great High Priest? It consisted in a complete dedication of himself to the Father and the Father's will. It found its most perfect expression on Calvary where he gave himself to suffering and death for his Father's sake, but it filled his soul from the beginning. In life and in death he gave himself entirely to his Father.

In life and in death he gave himself unreservedly also to mankind. There is no contradiction here, for Christ's giving of himself to men finds both its basis and its measure in his total dedication to the Father.

Here, as always, he is our model. We too, to the extent that we belong to God, can give ourselves fruitfully to men. To belong to God is, then, the fundamental ideal at which we must aim. Our work for souls will be Christlike—and therefore fruitful—only if it rests on that foundation.

That then is the proper order: dedication of ourselves to God and, arising from that, a giving of ourselves to souls. Christ himself put the same truth in different words when he told us that, if we wish to bear fruit, we must abide in him. At the last supper, when he ordained his first priests, he gave them an address which we may fairly describe as an ordination sermon. And it is surely significant that his whole emphasis in that discourse is on the importance of abiding in him, of union with him. To their work for souls, he makes, apart from the general precept of charity, hardly any reference at all.

A Christlike dedication of ourselves to God and to souls for God's sake, is therefore the very definition of a priestly life. This means self-sacrifice on a heroic scale; we cannot at the same time give ourselves to God and souls, and keep ourselves for ourselves. That is neither new nor surprising. The way of Christ was the way of the cross, and if we are to be other Christs, it must likewise be ours.

Perfection in this offering of ourselves is the work of a lifetime, but even though we only succeed in recognizing and regretting our lack of generosity, there is still great hope for us. When, however, we are satisfied with our offering, then there is danger of stagnation and decay. Perhaps the comment of a very wise spiritual writer on self-sacrifice in general may help us to realize in what direction our efforts should tend. Father John Grou S.J., the author of *A Manual for Interior Souls*, writes as follows: 'The first fruit of our devotion to God should be the union of our hearts with the adoration and annihilation of Jesus in his Mother's womb. When we give ourselves to God, it is unfortunately too often with a view to becoming something great, something distinguished, pride and self-love exercising a strong influence over our dedication to God.' A little self-examination, a little sincerity, will soon show us how true this is of much of our spiritual life. Consciously or unconsciously, it is ourselves we are seeking; our search for God is subordinated to our self-seeking. This defect can be removed partly by our own efforts with the help of ordinary grace; its complete removal requires the operation of God's special purifications. But the first step for us is to recognize the ill. We may perhaps be helped to realize how far we fall short by Father Grou's exhortation, for he continues: 'Let us now give ourselves to God with no other view than to be entirely consumed and destroyed, with no other desire than to sacrifice for ever all self-esteem, all anxiety for our exaltation—even our spiritual exaltation —all views, considerations and reflections connected with self. Let us once and for all lose sight of ourselves, and give up our being to God alone.'[1] This is a high ideal, but not too high for one who is rightly called *alter Christus*.

There are, however, many considerations which may help us to adopt this high ideal and to live up to it. One such consideration is the fact that our Lord, in calling us to the holiness of the priesthood, has already merited for us, at the cost of his precious Blood, all the graces and helps that are necessary for us to achieve it. If we are content to adopt and to follow an ideal lower than one which corresponds to his intentions we are frustrating him, we are nullifying his efforts, we are bringing to naught plans which he had so much at heart that he suffered and died for their achievement.

Perhaps, however, we are not exactly content with our low standards of aim and of achievement, but we see no possibility of doing any better. The fundamental source of this error—for it is an error and a very serious one—is our lack of true theological hope and a corresponding tendency to base our hopes on ourselves rather than on God. Even the apostles were not immune from this error. Time and time again our Lord reproached them with their lack of faith and confidence in him. 'Modicae fidei, quare dubitasti?' To us as to them our Lord addresses his assurances: 'With men, it is impossible; but not with God. For all things are possible with God.'[2] 'All things are possible to him that believeth.'[3] And St. Paul assures us: 'I can do all things in him who strengtheneth me.'[4] So far from indicating an early limit to our hope of progress, our knowledge of our limitations is rather a first and almost an essential condition for our progress. For our hope is in God, especially in God's mercy; and our holiness is to be the work of God. If we realize that, then we can say with St. Paul: 'Gladly therefore will I glory in my infirmities, that the power of Christ may dwell in me.'[5] His grace is sufficient for us, and power is perfected in infirmity. Our mistake lies in asking ourselves what *we* can do, instead of what *God* is willing to do. Once we are sure of our vocation to holiness, and for priests St. Pius X has left no room for doubt about that, the question of difficulty or impossibility does not arise; God's grace is sufficient for the carrying out of his wishes, and he himself will provide for all things necessary.

There is another approach to the problem which should be of great help. Not only is it a fact that our holiness is to come from Christ, but it is to come from Christ already present within our souls. This doctrine

of the divine indwelling is too often forgotten or overlooked. Yet there are few doctrines which offer such
consolation or such encouragement to the priest in his
pursuit of holiness. There is no need to prove to a
priest that God is really present in the soul of the just
man. The doctrine is obvious to anyone who reads St.
Paul. It should be still more obvious to any priest who
reflects on the theology of the sacrament of the Blessed
Eucharist. If the reception of the Body and Blood of
Christ under the form of food and drink signifies the
effect of the Blessed Sacrament, what must be the
intimate union with God which it produces? Too often
we think of Holy Communion as a wonderful means of
gaining a few minutes' temporary intimacy with the
human nature of Christ. We forget that its real purpose
is to nourish our intimacy with the divine nature of the
Son of God, to increase our share in that divine nature.
The doctrine of God's presence in our soul, connected
as it is with the doctrines of the Blessed Trinity and of
the Incarnation, is so rich and so many-sided that it
can be viewed in various ways. Let us here consider
it, as Fr. de Jaegher S.J. does in his book *One with
Jesus*, as the presence of Christ in our souls and our
identification with him. One fundamental effect of this
point of view, and of the devotion to which it leads,
is that we gradually cease to make ourselves the centre
of our lives and that we more and more make Christ
the centre. For Christ does not dwell in our souls in
order that we should live our own life through him,
for ourselves, so to speak, but rather that he may
continue his life in us, through us, for the sake of the
Father. We must not forget that the Persons of the
Blessed Trinity are essentially related and referred to one
another; each one is *ad alium*. For in the human life

of the Son, as we insisted earlier in this chapter, he lived and worked *propter patrem*. It is easy then to see how fundamental in the life of Christ is this utter dedication of himself to the Father; his dedication of his life to the souls of men is secondary to that and is both animated and controlled by it.

This dedication to the Father must find its counterpart in the life of the priest, who is another Christ and who so often offers the sacrifice of Christ. Our appointment to apostolic activity and our zeal for souls does not excuse us or exempt us from it. In fact it would seem that precisely because of our duty to souls, our duty of dedication to God becomes still more urgent and important. It was not by preaching but by his Passion and Death that Christ redeemed men. It would be a great mistake to think that we priests are called only to continue his work of preaching. Far from that, it is true rather that he is called us to allow him to continue in us his life of devotion to the Father. It follows, therefore, that there can be no true partnership with him, no genuine intimacy with him in our souls, unless we wish, at least, to share this fundamental sentiment of his heart. Too often our zeal is concentrated on doing things for God. Obviously that is a holy and wholesome purpose, provided that it be properly animated by divine charity. But it can become so predominant in our lives that we forget two important truths. The first is that the only things that are properly done for God are those that are done by Christ—either in himself or through us. The second is that in our own lives the things that God does to and for us are far more important, even for God, than the things we do for him. The whole of the later stages of purification in the mystical life seem to be aimed at convincing the soul that it has nothing and can do nothing, that in fact God is its All. But even in the earlier stages, it is important to realize how primary a part is played in it all by God. And for a priest, whether in his private life or in his apostolic work, it is still more important to realize this fact. There is only one person who can love God adequately, who can adore God properly, who can serve God exactly as he should be served: and that is Christ. Our work as priests is to put on Christ, to form him in ourselves and in those committed to our care.

All our efforts, then, should be aimed at allowing Christ to live in us and to share all our actions. All virtue, all perfection, all achievement should be sought principally as a means to this end. May we in passing here note a view of the spiritual life that is only too common among religious and which seems to be shared by many priests. It was very well put by one nun who said to the writer that they were taught that the important thing was to collect virtues; when you had a complete collection, like a lot of little parcels properly tied up and arranged, then possibly God might take some more personal interest in you and you might dare to hope for some slight degree of personal contact with him. Obviously from one point of view the doctrine is sound. But considered as a comprehensive view of even the approach to the spiritual life it is so utterly inadequate as to be a grotesque—one might almost say —perversion of the truth. The spiritual life begins in Baptism, with the entrance of the Holy Spirit into the soul and the incorporation of the soul in Christ. What can be more intimate than that? All that follows is a mere flowering of that divine seed, divinely sown. Christ is the beginning and the end. It is he to whom we owe our spiritual life and its development. It is upon him that we must rely, not on our own efforts or achievements.

However, in this matter it is not easy to write in general terms. We are not correcting ideas that are completely erroneous, we are merely indicating their inadequacy. It is not so much a question of truth or error as one of proper perspective. We have, of course, a part to play ourselves, an essential one. But the part played by Christ is far more important, and too much forgotten. For us priests anyhow, who can exercise our priestly functions only by the power of God, there is less excuse for overlooking the importance of Christ in our own spiritual lives, or in the service of the Father. If we could fashion an ideal and form a purpose of giving ourselves completely to him in every action, that he might use us to live his life of love and service of the Father, our whole lives would be changed and enriched. For we must remember, when we give ourselves to Christ, he also gives himself to us, and his merits are ours. This is one point where the limitations of the self-centred soul become evident. When such a person realizes that he has sinned, he immediately becomes discouraged, for he feels that his only hope of recovery and of progress lies in his being able to make personal satisfaction for his failings. Whereas the Christ-centred soul immediately seizes on the merits of Christ and offers them to the Father to propitiate him and to atone for its sins, and then goes on with its hope in God undiminished and unaffected. It is true he tries to make up to Christ by additional love and humility in the future. But his hope is not dependent on his efforts to make reparation. So too with difficulties. The self-dependent soul is discouraged by difficulties, and sets its course or lowers its purpose to avoid them. The Christ-centred soul merely makes certain that the way which these difficulties beset is really the way Christ wishes it to proceed. Once reassured on this point, it gaily goes ahead, quite confident in the power and the will of Christ to deal with these difficulties. But these are only examples. The whole life and outlook of a soul centred on Christ differ *toto coelo* from those of the soul centred on itself.

It is true that the perfection of this Christocentric outlook belongs to the more mature stages of the spiritual life. But from the very beginning the life of the Christian must in its essentials be centred on Christ. This is still more true of the life of a priest. Notwithstanding all appearances to the contrary, it is equally true of the *work* of the priest, for Christ insists not only that we shall bear fruit if we abide in him, but also that if we do not abide in him, we *shall not* bear fruit. That is why we are so insistent on the need for an interior life in the priest called to apostolic labours. There is no other way in which he can achieve success in the apostolate. That is why, too, we put before priests devotion to Christ living in their own souls, as an ideal. It will not only promote their personal progress but it will also fertilize their work for souls.

One practice that may help us to develop an appreciation of Christ's presence within us is the habit of a daily visit, if one may so call it, to Christ present in our souls. And perhaps this 'visit' would be all the more successful if it were made not in the church, but somewhere in private. By a 'visit', we merely mean a turning of our attention to Christ represented as present within us, and a short converse with him, something after the manner of our thanksgiving after Holy Communion. We should be careful, in our converse with him, to stress our need for his co-operation in all our actions, and our willingness to be guided by him in all things. We should of course earnestly ask him to make us conformable to himself, to animate us with his views, and to unite us every day more closely to himself. But it would be fatal to think that this is a devotion that is limited to a particular practice or set of practices. It is essentially a devotion that must gradually occupy our whole lives, so that we come to live and act with Christ, for Christ and through Christ. One consoling thought in this regard is that our Lord is intensely eager to produce this union of heart and mind, of life and activity. All we have to do is to cease interfering with his efforts. And after our Lord, no one is more interested or more anxious about it than our Lady. If we approach her for her Son's sake she will certainly work wonders to transform our souls. But we must not forget our Father who is in heaven; for his whole Providence is intent on uniting us to his Son, so that abandonment to his will is the key-note of this devotion, as it was the key-note of the life of Christ.

[1] *The Interior of Jesus and Mary*
[2] Mark X, 27
[3] Mark IX, 22
[4] Phil. IV, 13
[5] 2 Cor. XII, 9

CHAPTER EIGHTEEN

THE HOLY GHOST IN OUR SOUL

IT is difficult, as most priests will agree, to treat adequately of the Holy Ghost and to give practical advice about devotion to him. But, if difficult, it is essential, for we cannot overlook the importance which our Lord attached to the Holy Spirit whom he was to send to us.

In fact, when reading the Gospels, we often get the impression that this sending of the Holy Spirit into our souls is the crowning purpose of Christ's life and death. 'I tell you the truth: it is expedient to you that I go: for if I go not, the Paraclete will not come to you; but if I go, I will send him to you.'¹ This thought loomed large in his mind at the last supper, when he prayed for the sending of the Holy Spirit on his apostles. 'I will ask the Father, and he shall give you another Paraclete, that he may abide with you for ever.'² So important is this gift of the Holy Spirit that St. Paul can say, speaking by the same Holy Spirit: 'If any man have not the Spirit of Christ, he is not of his.'³ We cannot, then, let any inherent difficulties deter us from attempting to achieve some knowledge and devotion in regard to this Gift of God.

Who, then, is this Holy Spirit? First of all, he is God himself, the third Person of the Blessed Trinity. Now this third Person 'proceeds' in the Blessed Trinity by

way of love, so that one may say that he is the very
love with which God loves himself. Or, to be more
accurate, he is the very love with which the Father and
the Son love one another. St. Thomas bluntly says:
'The Holy Ghost is the love of the Father and the Son.'[4]
It is true that he discusses at length the exact ways in
which it may be said that the Father and the Son love
one another 'by the Holy Spirit',[5] but having determined the exact meaning to be attached to the phrase,
he would even include *us* in the object so loved. We
may then borrow a phrase from St. John of the Cross
and call the Holy Ghost 'the living flame of divine love.'

Now we know that in the Blessed Trinity all is
common to the three Persons where there is no opposition of relation. The same one intelligence, the same
one will, the same one power, the same one majesty is
common to each Person, because the same one and
indivisible divine nature is common to the three Persons.
So too all exterior works, that is, all those actions
accomplished 'outside' God, whether in the material
world or in the souls of men, all these are common to
the three divine Persons, since it is the one divine nature
that is the principle of all such works. But the Church
deliberately attributes certain actions to individual
Persons because of some affinity between the operation
and the property of that Person. The Creed professes
our belief in the omnipotent Father, the Creator of
Heaven and earth, and all works in which the power
of God is especially manifest are generally attributed to
the Father. So, too, works in which the divine wisdom
is prominent, such as the order and arrangement of the
universe, are attributed by way of appropriation to the
Son. Since the Holy Ghost is so intimately connected
with divine love, to him are appropriated the works in

which the divine love and goodness are especially expressed, particularly the work of God's loving mercy in the sanctification of our souls. Our Lord's own words can themselves be used to justify this principle of appropriation and the scriptures definitely attribute to the Holy Ghost the pouring out of grace and charity into our souls. This is not done without reason, and we cannot neglect the role so divinely attributed to the Holy Spirit without great loss to ourselves. Let us consider for a moment what the Holy Spirit does to our souls.

He comes to us as the Gift of God and makes his abode with us. He elevates our souls to a superhuman state and transforms them by sanctifying grace. He endows them with the fundamental virtues of faith, hope and charity, enriches them with the moral virtues and adorns them with his sevenfold gifts. It is of the highest importance for us to have some realization of this indwelling of the Holy Spirit in our souls and of his work there. We are, indeed, familiar with the tremendous divine intimacy conferred on us in Holy Communion when Christ gives us his Body and Blood under the sacramental species, and remains intimately present with us as long as the species endure. We know, of course, that he is not inactive while he is with us; we realize that he gives us many wonderful graces. But we may feel that when this sacramental presence has ceased, the time of personal intimacy and union with the divinity is over. Moreover, when we think of the sacramental Christ present within us, we have a tendency to think mainly of his human nature, and we have a certain difficulty in forming any image which effectively represents and suggests intimate union with him. In fact, if we try to be *too* clear or definite in our imagery, the notion of intimate union with God may become not only difficult but even impossible to maintain. So that although our Lord's words to his disciples telling them that it was expedient for them that he should go referred to his Ascension and to the effects that would follow, yet they are not without significance even in this context. And although it is by the humanity of Christ that the divinity is revealed to us, yet it was not without reason that Christ himself warned us of our need of the Spirit, for it is in the unity of the Spirit that we are made one with him. It is of importance, then, that we give devotion to the Holy Ghost its proper place in our lives. Otherwise we shall miss much of the fruit of the Passion and Death of our Saviour.

The difficulty of forming a concept of the third Person is a real one. The second Person is known to us in his humanity and in the Sacrament of his love. Even in regard to the first Person, his name of Father establishes him in our hearts and appeals to one of our fundamental instincts. But the name of the Holy Ghost appeals to no familiar experience. Yet the very vagueness and obscurity that it conveys leaves us more freedom and facility to conceive a close personal union. At the very least it removes apparent obstacles that can arise from the images we form in the case of the other two Persons.

To describe the Holy Ghost as the soul of our soul could, of course, be completely wrong, if we take the word soul too literally. Yet he has been called the soul of the Mystical Body of Christ, and also his role has been compared to that of the heart in the human body. These two descriptions will give us some idea of the intimacy and the permanence of his presence within us.

Before, however, we try to explain something of the truth they contain, it may be no harm to note two points that can affect and impair our grasp of this truth. In his admirable work on the Holy Ghost, the late Fr. Edward Leen points them out. The first point is this. Owing perhaps to the controversy with the first Protestants, and the dispute about the value of good works, great emphasis has been laid on the moral aspect of religion. The theology of human acts and their efficacy for salvation have been so stressed since the time of the Reformation that, as Fr. Leen says, the average mind has got the idea that morality is the principal element of the supernatural life. The fact is, of course, that morality is only a condition of the supernatural life. Human conduct takes the primary place, instead of the extraordinary elevation of the human being by the divine contact. We must restore the primacy of place to the divine in our spiritual life and devotion to the Holy Ghost is a most effective way of doing it.

The second point which Fr. Leen emphasizes is this. From our very early days we have been accustomed to the idea that God is everywhere. For many of us, unfortunately, this idea conjured up a picture of a watchful and critical overseer, a just but inflexible judge, always waiting to catch us doing wrong and to punish us for it. There may be a tendency to carry over this idea of God into our relations with the Holy Ghost. Unless we can correct this tendency we will find it very difficult to be at ease with our divine Guest, and our inclination will be to neglect and forget him.

In order to obtain a more correct view, it may help us to remember that the Holy Ghost is sent and given to us by the Father and the Son and that they send him to us as a result of their concern for sinners. We have two significant pictures of their attitude to sinners. The Son, who was given the name of Jesus because he was to save his people from their sins, describes himself as the Good Shepherd who leaves the ninety-nine other sheep in order to find the one that was lost. And when he has found it, he puts it tenderly on his shoulders, rejoicing. The Father is shown to us in the parable of the prodigal son as a father who runs to meet his repentant child, embraces him, clothes him, restores all he has lost and makes a feast for his return. Surely, then, we need have no servile fear of the third Person whom these two send us and who himself is the remission of our sins. Our Lord has told us that the Holy Spirit comes to supply for his own absence, as another paraclete to console and strengthen us. The yoke his presence lays upon us is, like the yoke of Christ, easy and the burden is light. He comes to us with all the loving tenderness and compassion of the all-merciful God—for he is God himself.

So far from being in our souls to condemn us, he is there to regenerate us. He has justified us and continues to sanctify us. As St. Thomas says: 'The gift of sanctifying grace is not given to us in order that we may have no further need of divine help; every creature requires to be preserved by God in the good already received from him . . . For that reason the work of the Holy Spirit is not limited by the effect of his permanent gifts in us; apart from this effect, he moves and guides us yet more.'[6] He is continually giving us light and strength. Of old, God promised by his prophet: 'I will give you a new heart, and put a new spirit within you; and I will take away the stony heart out of your flesh, and give you a heart of flesh.

And I will put my spirit in the midst of you: and I will cause you to walk in my commandments, and to keep my judgments, and do them.'[7] We can easily apply these words to the work of the Holy Spirit within us, which indeed is well summed up in St. Paul's phrase that the Holy Spirit 'helpeth our infirmity.'[8] The Church underlines the benignity of his interest in us in her hymns. She addresses him: 'Pater pauperum, Dator munerum, Consolator optime, Dulcis hospes animae, Dulce refrigerium.' This wonderful prayer, the *Veni Sancte Spiritus*, is full of light on the tenderness of the Holy Ghost. 'In labore requies, In aestu temperies, In fletu solatium.' In this hymn too the Church makes it clear exactly what we are of ourselves and what he does for us, when she sings: 'Sine tuo numine, Nihil est in homine, Nihil est innoxium.' It is because of our utter helplessness that the Holy Spirit is given to us and that we must go to him with unshakeable confidence.

We should, then, pray frequently and fervently for devotion to the Holy Spirit and take care to make that devotion an intergal part of our spiritual lives. Further, we should try to realize to what great dignity he has raised us by making us participators in the divine nature. To live in accordance with that dignity we have continual need of his inspiration and his help. We cannot even pray without him; he, in fact, prays for us 'with unspeakable groanings.' We have already referred to the comparson of his work in our souls with that of the soul in the human body. The Holy Spirit cannot, of course, enter into a substantial union with our souls as the soul does with the body, But he can and does act as a vivifying principle upon which every single movement of our supernatural life depends, both for its inception and its execution. Without him we are dead, for all our spiritual life depends on him.

This fact should be at the basis of our devotion to him. We should turn to him almost instinctively in all our needs and ask for his help and guidance. As we grow in grace his inspirations and initiative become more evident. At no time, of course, does he deprive us of our liberty. There is, however, a difference in the manner of acting of the virtues and the gifts, and as we come nearer to God, the gifts are more in evidence. These make us so pliable in his hands that St. Thomas says that under their influence the human mind 'non se habet ut movens sed magis ut mota.' The Fathers sometimes have illustrated the difference by a comparison. Using the virtues we are like men rowing a boat by their own efforts, but under the influence of the gifts the boat is moved gently and speedily onward by the wind in its sail.

What we have to do in practice is to be very careful to conform to the inspirations of the Holy Spirit. Cardinal Manning sees three degrees of 'non-conformity' in three texts of scripture. 'Grieve not the holy Spirit of God';[9] 'You always resist the Holy Ghost'[10]; 'Extinguish not the spirit'.[11] These words of scripture should warn us of the danger of refusing to listen to his voice. For we can so harden our hearts that we no longer hear him, and he will then cease to speak to us. This, of course, is ruinous and is a fate that we must avoid at whatever cost. Our ideal should be the very opposite; we should strive to rely on and to be very attentive to him, for it is only when we are led and 'activated' by him in all things that we are living fully as sons of God.

Obviously we have a duty to reverence him present

in our souls, but this reverence should not prevent a loving familiarity. Theologians stress the fact that he is given to us as a *gift*; that is, he is ours for our use and enjoyment. We should, then, make use of him. In all our doubts and uncertainties we should turn to him for guidance. He may not speak to us directly but he will not leave us without guidance, for he has compassion on our infirmity. In difficulties and temptations we should appeal to him for strength and courage. He will aid our infirmity and strengthen us with his grace. We can make our own the Church's prayer to him: 'Lava quod est sordidum, Riga quod est aridum, Sana quod est saucium, Flecte quod est rigidum Fove quod est frigidum, Rege quod est devium.' He aids us by transforming us.

This 'use' of the Holy Ghost is of special significance at private prayer. When our prayer disappears in aridity and distraction, then we should realize that he is within us praying and that we have only to second his prayer in order to be pleasing to the Father. One of the great obstacles to progress in prayer and in the whole spiritual life is our tendency to make ourselves instead of God the centre of our supernatural strivings. We shall not succeed until we accept the failure of our own efforts and put all our confidence in God within us. In our prayer we should always remember that we have in the Holy Spirit the mutual Love of the Father and the Son as our own possession and that we can always offer the Father this divine Love. And if that attitude of prayer overflows into our lives, if we 'use' the Holy Spirit, we shall approach closely to the example of our Lord, who all his life was led by the Holy Spirit, who handed himself over completely to him and who thus always did the things that pleased his Father. That was Christ's way; it should be ours too, and there is no better way of pleasing God.

One other point is of particular significance for us priests. St. Paul tells us that it was by the Holy Spirit that Christ offered himself to God.[12] We, his priests, have to offer ourselves with him daily on the altar. We can do this, *sicut oportet*, only by the Holy Spirit. We should then frequently beg the Holy Ghost for the spirit of sacrifice. When we begin the Church's sacrifice, she puts on our lips, at the offering of the bread and wine, a prayer to the Holy Spirit. 'Veni sanctificator, omnipotens aeterne Deus.' It is true that this prayer has a special reference to the Eucharistic sacrifice. But we may use it to ask a blessing on the sacrifice of ourselves which we can and should make in the offering of the bread and wine. In the days of old, God sent down fire from heaven to consume the sacrifices offered to him. Today he sends down the Holy Spirit, the fire of divine love, into our hearts. If we would have our sacrifice of ourselves acceptable we must allow ourselves to be consumed by this divine fire, ever present, ever working, ever praying within us. There at the altar we priests can find a wonderful starting point for our daily lives, if we offer ourselves completely to God that his Holy Spirit may perfectly possess and animate us. Our Lord has told us that if we ask anything of the Father in his name it will be given to us, and he has specifically mentioned the Father's readiness to give the 'good Spirit' to those who ask him. Let us go, then, to the Father and remind him of the merits of his Son. Let us point out to him the Son's desire for our love and for our perfect service of the Father. Let us represent to him how completely the Son has deserved to be loved by us. Pleading our poverty and reminding him of his Son's promises, let us ask him to give us his Holy Spirit so that we may love his Son as his Son desires and deserves to be loved. That is a prayer that God cannot fail to hear and one which will bring down rich blessings on our souls.

[1] John XVI, 7
[2] John XIV, 16
[3] Rom. VIII, 9
[4] III, 32, 1
[5] Cf. I, 37
[6] I-IIae, 109, 9
[7] Exech. XXXVI, 26-27
[8] Rom. VIII, 26
[9] Ephes. IV, 30
[10] Acts VII, 51
[11] 1 Thess. V, 19
[12] Cf. Heb. IX, 14

CHAPTER NINETEEN

CHRIST THE LIFE OF THE SOUL

THERE is one point on which every priest should examine himself at intervals during his life. It is not easy to formulate the question exactly. One could approach the point by asking what spirit animates our life and work: the spirit of the world or the spirit of Christ? Each of us could ask himself: who is the centre of my life? Is it Christ or is it myself? Or we might formulate the question in a phrase previously used in these pages which, if lacking in dignity, at least emphasizes the point of the enquiry: am I more intent on delivering the goods than on delivering myself? Christ, the Holy Ghost tells us, did all things well, but above all he delivered himself.

None of these attempts to put the question quite meets the needs of each individual situation but they help to remind us of the necessity for continual vigilance over the attempts of self-love and self-seeking to intrude into and even to take charge of our priestly lives. Our Lord has laid down self-renunciation as an essential condition of being his disciples. And however generously or however thoroughly we renounced self at the beginning of our priesthood, it is, first of all, like a weed that continually tends to return and overrun the garden unless constantly held in check; and also it is a matter which calls for new and further efforts at different stages of our progress.

As a preliminary to our discussion let us note what seems to be a general pattern frequently observable in the life of the soul. When a soul, under the influence of God's grace, first sets out in pursuit of holiness, there is nearly always a considerable degree of self in both the principle and the end of our efforts. Nevertheless God's grace is powerful and we do achieve something. But then he seems to decide that what we have built is not good enough and he pulls the whole edifice down, sometimes quite violently and painfully. If we behave as befits men of faith, hope and charity, we begin again in closer partnership with and in greater dependence on him, and we again achieve some success, this time of more value. But, again, our Lord seems not content and again our work is wrecked. This is a process or a pattern which may be repeated quite often in the life of a soul called to holiness. Sometimes the different chapters, so to speak, stand out in bold relief and the summits and the valleys are clear to the beholder. At other times the re-moulding and the remaking are not so obvious, for the process is more continuous and more even. But it is nonetheless real, nonetheless disconcerting —and nonetheless effective. It is well to keep this pattern in mind for it will help us to understand and accept much that is disconcerting and difficult in God's providence in our regard. It applies, of course, in the first place to our efforts at spiritual advancement, but it also applies to our work for God among souls.

To take the latter aspect of the matter first, it cannot be denied that there is frequently a good deal of self-seeking in the work of our ministry. Not all of it is culpable—some of it, in fact, at certain times is even praiseworthy. But sooner or later it has to be eliminated. It is amazing how many good works, begun in a true zeal for God's glory, can become dominated by a self-seeking that is truly pagan for all its facade of apostolic action. We have all heard of the famous preacher on his deathbed whose friends were trying to console him and remove his fear of God's judgement by reminding him of the great sermons he had preached. His answer, 'If God does not refer to those sermons I shall take care not to remind him', shows a deathbed revaluation of a life's work that may well be our own if we are not a little more critical of our motives. Preaching, for example, if a man has a special talent for it, can easily be the occasion of much self-seeking. The truly apostolic man preaches the word of God in order to bring souls to God. As he grows in grace he becomes more and more animated by the dispositions of the heart of Jesus, and his desire to satisfy the longing of that heart for the love of men becomes the driving motive of his preaching. But unfortunately it is possible to let other motives come with us to the pulpit. We may find ourselves preaching ourselves, not Jesus Christ. We may become more interested in showing our talents than in drawing men to our Saviour. Worldly fame, 'the bubble reputation in the fool's mouth', may even become our aim, and it is not unknown that men will preach to entertain rather than to edify. Such self-seeking, however, is generally quite obvious, and unless a man has become completely impervious to the protests of conscience and the comments of his colleagues, he will soon have to admit and to remedy the error of his ways.

But there are more dangerous forms of self-seeking

in the ministry. In our work we can aim at and achieve a success which seems directed to God's glory, which excites the commendation of our superiors, the praise and perhaps the envy of our colleagues. Yet the whole thing can be vitiated by a secret worship and seeking of self that makes all our activity a devotion to our own glory rather than to the glory of God. Even such works as the conversion of non-believers or the reform of sinners can be animated by motives that are centred on ourselves. There is, however, more danger of a deviation where the work we have to do is less directly concerned with the service of souls, such, for example, as the building of churches, the raising of funds, or the organization of some outstanding enterprise or function. In all these cases, what makes the position so invidious is that the work is the work allotted to us by authority—it is God's will. And our success is also what authority hopes for and commends. It is easy to fool ourselves under such circumstances and to blind ourselves to the fact that love of ourselves, not love of God, is the mainspring of our activity. And that is such a tragedy! For if we do all these things without charity, they profit us nothing—and we *are* nothing.

The general pattern of a 'priestly' life is determined fairly clearly by regulations and clerical conventions. These restraints on our freedom can, no doubt, be irksome, but many of us can adapt ourselves fairly easily to the mould. For some of us such a life is even congenial; for others it presents no great difficulty. But inside the limits laid down by such a life a man can do his whole work as a priest in much the same spirit as laymen carry on their professions or pursue their careers. And to make it more dangerous, many of the principles of conduct imposed by the demands of a priestly life are almost identical with the dictates of worldly prudence in the pursuit of a career. The avoidance of mistakes, continual circumspection in conduct, due submission to authoirty, careful restraint in speech, assiduity in work, promptness in perfor- mance, correctness of bchaviour: all such have to be observed by the careerist as well as by the man of God. I do not say the difference is not noticeable, for ambition will in the long run betray itself, but the resemblance can be an occasion of self-deceit for the unfortunate man who tries to persuade himself that his devotion to self is really devotion to God. The desire for ad- vancement, for fame, for self can possess the heart of a priest just as it can possess the heart of a layman, and the pursuit of such desires can disguise itself, at least with some success, as rcal prudence or charity to one's own family or in many other ways. We have always to be on our guard against becoming the victims of such self-seeking.

Not only in our work for others, but even in the effort to perfect ourselves and to acquire holiness, the influence of self-seeking can be considerable. A priest could seek supernatural perfection in a spirit very much akin to that in which an artist seeks to perfect natural talent. There is a world of difference between the search for holiness for our own sake and the desire to be holy for God's sake. It is important to recognize the fact that sclf-sccking can, and in the initial stages usually does, play a part in our desire to advance in spirituality. But it is equally important to be very prudent and cautious in all attempts to remedy this condition. In fact, to some extent, such self-seeking, far from being blameworthy, is actually quite praiseworthy and even necessary. As one progresses, the part played by it has to decrease and the ultimate removal of the defects caused by self-love is really the work of God. But even though in the beginning self-seeking can have its proper place, it very often leads to excesses and exaggerations that make difficulties not only for oneself but also for others. In a book called *The Salt of the Earth*,[1] which we heartily recommend to every priest, Fr. S. M. Shaw paints a striking but sympathetic picture of this conflict between nature and grace. He describes a young priest who feels called to advance beyond the apparent mediocrity of his colleagues. He does not frown at the amusements indulged in by his friends, but he feels that *he* is above such things. In his efforts to avoid appearing to condemn the comparative laxity of his companions, his expression assumes a sweetness that shows his tolerance for such self-indulgence. But when the critical comments of his neighbours come to his ears, the realization that he is sharing in the saints' lot of being misunderstood and even persecuted leads to such an intensification and etherealization of the sweetness of his expression that his colleagues become infuriated. The good young man is perfectly in earnest and perfectly sincere. Yet his friends are not altogether mistaken in feeling that there is a good deal of self-seeking in his conduct. Grace, eventually, will enlighten him and the value of the canon that frowns on singularity may manifest itself to him. But all such happenings are really only different symptoms of the one fundamental disease: the failure to make Christ the centre of the spiritual life and of all apostolic work.   It is not easy to correct errors of perspective without falling into exaggeration or such overstatement as would lead to new errors. It is perfectly true that in our apostolate we have to serve God, to do things for him, to labour in his vineyard. It is perfectly true that in the spiritual life we have to aim at and labour for our own perfection. We have to fight the good fight, we have to earn heaven as the reward of our good work and merit eternal beatitude by our own acts. Yet, true as all that is, it is far less than half the truth. In the first place, everything that we have to do is supernatural—completely beyond our powers—and therefore it can be done only by God's help. Has he not himself reminded us that without him we can do nothing? In the second place, our capacity 'to do things for God' and our power to merit are the gratuitous gifts of God's mercy. He has no need of us except in so far as he may wish to allow the outcome of some of his plans to depend on our co-operation. And if he does thus make us of some importance in his plans, it is because he has compassion on our infirmities and, in his generous love, wishes to give us some opportunity of adding to what he has in store for us the relish of having, in some measure, earned it. Christ could save every soul in the world without a single priest. If he does not choose to do so but decides to make us ministers in the work of Redemption, it is solely because he wishes to share with us his happiness and his crown. If he makes us his servants, it is because he has quite gratuitously chosen to make us his friends. The same principle applies to our own spiritual lives. It is not we who perfect ourselves; our sanctification is the work of God. And if he lets his work involve our co-operation, it is only because his loving kindness wants to clothe his gifts with the mantle of rewards. There is only one mediator between God and men: Christ Jesus. And we will never be true apostles until we realize that our function is to let him use us just as he wills in the work of mediation, always remembering that we are but helpless instruments in his hands. There is only one spiritual life and that is the life of Christ. And we can never begin to be saints until we realize that all sanctity consists in the replacing of ourselves and our lives by Christ and the life of Christ. *He* is the life of our souls. Therefore the sooner we die to ourselves, the sooner he will live in us.

Let us add to that two very important principles. The first is that while God created the world and rules the world for his own glory, he intends *in this life* to glorify himself by his mercy. It would seem that the glory of his justice refers more to the next life. Here below mercy is the predominant attribute which animates all his works. The second principle is this. In all his dealings with our souls here below Jesus is always a Saviour and is always acting as such. Until we realize this and adopt in all sincerity and cheerful willingness the attitude of one who needs continually to be saved, we are not in our true relationship to God nor are we living as we should.

In what we have written we have merely pointed out the fairly obvious fact that self-seeking can easily intrude into our spiritual lives and our apostolic work. We have not sought to give any detailed analysis of the matter nor—and at this the reader may be surprised— have we discussed how we are to get rid of the intruder. Our reason for leaving the subject without any practical discussion of the counter-measures to be taken is that in the long run we think that the fewer counter-measures we take, the better! Frankly, we think that this battle against self is a battle which, to some extent at any rate, is better fought by not fighting and more easily won by running away. That, obviously, requires some elucidation, for the classical spiritual tradition is rightly insistent on depicting the spiritual life as a war against self. But who is going to conduct this war? If it is our *self*, then victory only means a further exaltation of self, and the attention to self necessary for the fight is about the worst way to forget self. The answer to the paradox is that the proper way to deal with self is to forget self altogether and go to Jesus. If we concentrate our attention on him we will forget ourselves; if we hand over our work to him, he will soon accomplish our death to ourselves and bring us to a new life in himself.

The one thing, then, that is really necessary for the priest who wishes to fulfil his vocation is to study Christ, to talk to Christ, to know Christ, to seek Christ, to put on Christ and to love Christ with every fibre of his being. Our Lord himself had no other counsel for his apostles on the night he made them priests than to insist that he was the Vine, they the branches, that they could bear fruit only by abiding in him and that to abide in him was all that was necessary in order to bring forth fruit. All his disciples must leave themselves and follow him. To the mother of the two apostles who wanted the chief posts in his kingdom for her sons, he had nothing better to offer than that they should drink the chalice of which he was to drink unto death. To anyone who reads the New Testament in a proper frame of mind, every page is eloquent of the truth that we can reach eternal life only by dying to ourselves.

Yet when we start to live a spiritual life our whole preoccupation is with ourselves. We become meticulous in the scrutiny of our actions; we spend our energy in planning the details of our programme and worrying over our policy. Our hope is measured by what we see in ourselves—if not what we actually see, at least what we see potentially. Everything has to be merited or bought from God. In fact, we see ourselves as the principle and purpose of our sanctification. Now, we cannot altogether be blamed for that. There is much in our surroundings, in all that we see and hear, to help us to form that view. But it is, of course, a completely mistaken view. After all, as St. Thomas says in discussing sacrifice: 'By sacrifice we show the ordering of our mind to God. For the right ordering of our mind to God it is necessary that we should recognize that all we have is from God as a first principle and should be directed to God as to the ultimate end.' And we, as priests, offer sacrifice daily! As priests too, we preach the theological virtue of hope. We tell our people that they should hope in God *because God is good*, but in actual fact our own hope is rather in ourselves because we are—or expect to be—good. Once, however, we grasp the glorious truth, everything is changed. For our title to the kingdom of heaven is no longer our own pretended riches but our spiritual poverty— as our Lord told us it should be. Then we begin to glory in our infirmities, for virtue is made perfect in infirmity and God's grace is sufficient for us. Our sufficiency in fact is from God.

That is why it is so important to get away from ourselves as quickly and as completely as we can. And we will never understand God's dealings with our souls until we realize that they are based on this need for getting rid of self and replacing that self by God. God may draw us at first by condescending to make use of our self-love. He may show us the sweetness of his service and the charm of his companionship. But then he withdraws these concessions to our self-seeking.

Our work goes wrong; it is misunderstood; we meet with criticism, with opposition and with failure. God seems to have let us down even where the good of others is concerned. And the desolation in our spiritual life is still more complete. We can no longer pray. Our exercises of piety are at best a dull weary routine and may even be an intolerable burden. Spiritual books are distasteful, even painfully so. The Bible commands a certain respect, but not much more. Hope: the very word is a mockery. Like the two disciples going down to Emmaus, our hope is in the past tense: 'We had hoped . . . !' And our desolation is akin to that of Job on his dunghill. Blind that we are, we cannot see that that is the most glorious assurance we can possibly have. The story of Job is the story of every soul that is to reach sanctity: there is no other way. It behoved Christ to suffer and to die and to enter into his glory and *there is no other way for us*. Until we are brought to nothing and accept that nothingness, we cannot be men after God's heart, for Christ cannot live in us.

At first sight, then, the war on self would seem to be our most important contribution to the work of our sanctification. That, however, is a view which we cannot quite accept, for at least two reasons. Firstly, as we have said, self may find still more food for its own exaltation in such a warfare. Secondly, no sane human being will let go of the only plank he has until he is convinced that the surrounding ocean will support him. No reasonable man can be expected to discard self until he learns Christ and is sure that he can cast his burden on him. That is why we feel that the most important thing for us to do is to build up a proper idea of Jesus, of his love for us, of his constant care for us, of his unlimited willingness to help us and to save us.

And we also feel justified in saying that when things go wrong or appear to have gone wrong—at any period of the spiritual life—whether it be a falling into mortal sin or the deprivation of some extraordinary grace, there is always the same sovereign remedy, that of casting our burden on the Lord, of abandoning ourselves to Jesus. Sins are terrible things. They matter fearfully, for they crucify Jesus. But in another sense they do not matter at all, for if we are sorry for them Jesus can and will save us from them. They will be no obstacle to our close friendship with him but will even be used by him for our benefit. Discouragement is one of the most dangerous diseases of the soul and one which can occur at any period of the spiritual life. Yet it is nearly always due to the same cause: too much regard of ourselves and too little regard of Jesus. Once the cause is known the remedy is obvious. Scruples have much in common with discouragement. While they do present a special problem which needs sympathetic and understanding treatment, the ultimate remedy is recourse to Jesus. In this case, however, the psychological obstacles to such a recourse must be removed. The same remedy is the only remedy for all self-centred piety. And it is the absolute necessity for the replacement of the self by Christ that is at the root of all God's dealings with the soul. We have been told we must die in order to live. We have been told that we must leave ourselves and follow Christ. We have been told that we must be made new creatures in Christ. Why, then, worry about ourselves? Let us take God at his word and cast our burden upon his Son, cleaving to him who is our sufficiency, who is not only *our* all but even all the glory of God.

[1] Burns, Oates and Washbourne

CHAPTER TWENTY

THE SACRED HEART

IF we were asked what is the most important thing, in practice, in a priest's life, we should unhesitatingly say that it is his personal relationship with our Lord; and if we were asked what seems to be the most common short-coming in the spiritual life of priests, the answer would just as unhesitatingly be: the lack of personal intimacy with our Lord.

For priests engaged in the active apostolate, there is a danger of allowing preoccupation with their work in the Lord's vineyard to lessen their personal intimacy with the Master of the vineyard himself. If the process goes far enough, a stage can even be reached when the active priest no longer thinks of such intimate union with our Lord as essential, or even primary, in his vocation, but regards it as something characteristic rather of the cloister.

This is a grave misunderstanding of the vocation of the priest in the world. If ever men were called to the active life, the Apostles were. Yet throughout our Lord's address to them, his first priests, at the last supper the emphasis is always on love and union as a basis of their active apostolate, rather than on activity itself. They were to bear fruit, yes, but only on condition that they, the branches, remained united with him, the Vine. They would do great things for him, yes, but primarily and principally by abiding in him and in his love.

There was the same emphasis on love in the choosing of St. Peter as their head. We are all familiar with the words our Lord used to mark him out and give him supreme power of ruling the Church, but too many of us overlook the amazing significance of the threefold interrogation that preceded the threefold command to feed Christ's flock. In St. John's Gospel[1] we read of our Lord's insistent questioning of St. Peter: 'Simon, son of John, lovest thou me more than these?' The only qualification that our Lord asked St. Peter to manifest before making him head of the Church was outstanding love.

Again, the epistles of that other great Apostle, St. Paul, whose fiery spirit drove him all over the Roman world to preach Christ crucified, are overflowing with evidence that he was constantly and overpoweringly animated by love of Jesus, whom he had once persecuted. Certainly it was the charity of Christ that pressed him on to his supernal vocation.

It would be a tragic error both for ourselves and for our ministry if we failed to realize that what our Lord expected of the Apostles, his first priests, he expects also, with not a whit of difference, from every priest whom he has chosen.

The duty of the priest to seek perfection is clear from many Papal documents. It will be sufficient to cite Pope Pius XII in *Menti Nostrae*.[2] 'It must be recalled that even though the increasing needs of Christian society more urgently demand personal holiness in priests, they are already obliged by the very nature of the high ministry confided to them by God to work unceasingly for their own sanctification, always and everywhere.'

Moreover, the Holy Father makes it clear that, if this obligation is to be fulfilled, union with our Lord is of primary importance. 'The first striving of a priest should be for the closest union with the Divine Redeemer by accepting humbly and entirely the Christian doctrine and by diligently applying it in every moment of his life, so that his faith illumines his conduct and his conduct is the reflection of his faith. Led by the light of this virtue, let him keep his eyes fixed on Christ. Let him follow closely his teaching, his actions and his example, convincing himself that it is not sufficient for him to accomplish the duties enjoined on the ordinary faithful . . . The priestly life, since it arises from Christ, should always and in everything be directed towards him.'

There is a possible impediment to our whole-hearted pursuit of personal union with our Lord which should be noted here. The danger is a subtle one, for it arises from a misapplication of that study of right and wrong, of the precise boundary between the forbidden and the permissible, which necessarily occupied much of our attention in our seminary days, and which our ministry in the confessional must necessarily keep prominent in our minds as priests. The danger lies in carrying over into our own spiritual lives, as a proper and sufficient guide for ourselves, a criterion which was never meant for the purpose and is sadly inadequate to fulfil it. The mentality of the judge, of the canonist, is essential in its sphere; but we need to remember what that sphere is, and what are its limits. Beyond them, certainly, lies the field of generosity, of high sanctity as against mere avoidance of the pit, of the pursuit of the better and the best rather than the merely good. The judge's outlook, necessary as it is in much of our pastoral work, will not do when it is question of our own spiritual progress. It will at most tell us what we must do to serve without transgression; it will never show us how to serve as a lover serves. It will never lead us to that intimate union with our Lord which he expects of us.

There are indications that the importance of this personal union with our Lord needs special emphasis at the present time. There is in these days an extraordinary wealth of warnings and exhortations on this very point. Some are associated with private revelations, which must of course receive much sifting and testing; but the general reaction of the Church *discens* as well as *docens* seems to point to a special activity of the Holy Spirit in his desire to rekindle in men's hearts, and especially in priests' hearts, the fire of the love of God in and through Christ. Many of those whose work brings them into contact with a representative section of souls serving God notice an unusual willingness on God's part to pour out special graces of prayer and wisdom on everyone who comes, as one might say, even half-way to meet him. Again, in his providential action towards many whose zeal has borne much fruit in external works, but who—though 'good'—are far from understanding that their primary vocation is to love him, we notice what might almost be called a certain ruthlessness, as if he were bent on upsetting their successes and their talents. (An important feature of God's action in drawing souls to himself may be involved here; we shall consider the point later on).

The nature of the personal relationship our Lord expects of us is very clearly brought out in the devotion to the Sacred Heart, as explained in the writings of St. Margaret Mary, and especially as explained by Pope Pius XI in the Encyclical *Miserentissimus Deus* of 1928. The Lessons of the second Nocturn from Saturday to Thursday of the Sacred Heart octave consist of passages dealing with the Sacred Heart devotion taken from this Encyclical. The Latin of all but one of the passages we shall quote below will be found there.

We are chary, and rightly so, of private revelations as such, but the revelations claimed by St. Margaret Mary are put on a different footing by the unusual reference made to them by Pius XI. The devotion to the Sacred Heart, in any case, rests of course on the solidest of theological foundations, and is independent of the genuineness or otherwise of those revelations. However, the use Pius XI made of quotations from the Saint at least makes it clear that the sentiments attributed to our Lord in these passages may be taken as truly representing his attitude. Let us consider, then, what the Holy Father has written.

'When Jesus appeared to St. Margaret Mary, while emphasising the immensity of his love, he sorrowfully complained of the many insults committed against him by the ingratitude of men, in words that should be indelibly graven upon the hearts of the devout: "Behold" he said, "this heart that has so loved men and loaded them with benefits, but in return for its infinite love, far from finding any gratitude, has met only with neglect, indifference and insult, and these sometimes from souls that owe me a special duty of love."' A sentence of special importance for our present purpose is one in which it is emphasised that our Lord complains because his desires for our love are unrequited, rather than because his sovereign right to our service and

212

obedience is neglected: 'Our Lord revealed to that most pure disciple of his Sacred Heart, St. Margaret Mary, that, not so much in view of his rights over mankind, as by reason of his great love for us, he ardently desired that men should pay him this tribute of devotion.'

The frequent insistence, in the revelations described by St. Margaret Mary, on making reparation for the insults and outrages to which our Lord is subjected, may perhaps raise in our minds the question whether there is any conflict here with the doctrine of the present impassibility of Christ. If we have any un-easiness on the point—and it seems that some priests have—it should be put at rest once and for all, for it could hold us back from entering whole-heartedly into the full spirit of devotion to the Sacred Heart in particular, and in general into that whole field of heart-to-heart, friend-to-friend relationship with our Lord of which the Sacred Heart devotion is an out-standing expression. Here again Pius XI gives us safe and satisfying guidance.

'But how can it be said that Christ reigns blessed in heaven if he can be consoled by such acts of re-paration? We might answer in the words of St. Augus-tine: "A loving soul will understand what I say."[3] Everyone that is truly inflamed with the love of God turns his mind to the past, and sees him in the midst of most grievous torments, "for us men and for our salvation", afflicted by sorrow and anguish, weighed down with ignominy, "bruised for our sins", healing us by his stripes. He will meditate with the greater truth if he considers that the sins and iniquities of men, at whatsoever time committed, were the cause for which the Son of God was given up to death, and would of themselves even now cause the death of Christ, and a death accompanied by the same pains and anguish, since every sin can be regarded as in some manner renewing the Passion of our Lord, "crucifying again to themselves the Son of God, and making him a mockery."[4] If then in foreseeing the sins of the future the soul of Jesus became sorrowful unto death, it cannot be doubted that he already felt some comfort when he foresaw our reparation, when "there appeared to him an angel from heaven",[5] bearing consolation to his heart overcome with sorrow and anguish. Hence, even now, in a mysterious but true manner, we may, and should, comfort the Sacred Heart, continually wounded by the sins of ungrateful men: for Christ—as we also read in the Sacred Liturgy—complains by the mouth of the psalmist that he is abandoned by his friends: "My heart hath expected reproach and misery. And I looked for one who would grieve together with me, but there was none; and for one that would comfort me, and I found none"."[6]

The Holy Father goes on to speak of Christ's sufferings in his Mystical Body, and reminds us that 'Jesus Christ himself taught the same truth when to Saul, "as yet breathing out threatenings and slaughter against the disciples", he said: "I am Jesus whom thou persecutest." By these words he clearly meant that persecutions directed against the Church are a grievous attack upon her Divine Head. Christ, then, as he still suffers in his mystical body, rightly desires to have us as his companions in the work of expiation.'

It is perhaps possible to learn, in this matter, even from the enemy. We cite an example from our own experience. It is a horrible example, but its very horror may serve to impress on us how real and actual are the issues involved in our discussion. A most unfortunate woman, who had once communicated at a 'black mass', stated that she had to do what the devil urged her to do. This was to take the Sacred Host and desecrate it. Her life had been a most unhappy one, and she expressed great hatred of God for having allowed all that had happened to her. We asked her what satisfaction she could get from her actions, since Christ was now incapable of suffering, and in the Host she could only harm the species. Her answer came with readiness and complete sureness: 'Oh, I can still hurt him in Gethsemani!'

We have dealt with a number of possible misunderstandings or difficulties which might impede us in responding to that yearning our Lord has for our friendship, for our personal love. Yet, when all these have been set aside, it still remains true that many of us who sincerely want to make that response are quite discouraged by our lack of success. The lesson we have to learn is that we cannot set our own hearts on fire: this is a grace that God must give. Like the host of the wedding feast in the Gospel, God provides the wedding garment.

Our part is to ask, and the Mother of Fair Love is our obvious helper here. Let us draw her attention to our lack of wine; let us offer her the weak water of our desire and dispositions, and beg her—for her Son's sake—to get it changed into the wine of Divine Love. The answer will be, as it was at Cana: 'Whatever he shall say to you, that do ye.' Wherever his will is done, wherever his will is submitted to, there he is at work setting us on fire with the Flame of Divine Love; for God's whole plan in governing the world is to bring us to love his Son.

Our prayer must be sincere and humble—and insistent. We all know the example given by our Lord of the man who knocked up his neighbour at midnight for bread, and was heard not exactly for his reverence but for his importunity. We are familiar with the parable, but do we realize the full significance of the lesson our Lord draws from it? He tells us that if we ask and seek and knock we shall receive and find and be welcomed; and then he adds the golden words: 'If you then, being evil, know how to give good things to your children, how much more will your Father from heaven *give the good Spirit* to them that ask him?'[7]

This is the very Spirit we need, for it is in and by the Holy Ghost—who is Divine Love—that we are to love Jesus. This prayer should be daily on our lips: 'Father, for the sake of thy Son and because of his merits, give me thy Holy Spirit, so that I may love thy Son Jesus as he desires and deserves to be loved.' *Such a prayer must be heard.* It is based and centred on the Son, on his desires and his merits; and it asks for something which God clearly wills, and which he can give. We will certainly be answered.

But the answer may surprise us. Our Lord warned that his Father is a good husbandman and prunes the branches of his vine. We may find that things start to go wrong with us. It may be that our health suffers, and our abilities are impaired; that our friends seem to change, and our Superiors to misjudge us; that our plans go awry, our successes turn to failures. And we are in despair. We had hoped, yes, but we had hoped in our work, in our service, in our justice. And these things are being taken from us.

If we 'but knew the gift of God', we would sing an exultant *Te Deum*! God is forcing us to make two changes. Previously we were intent on doing things for God; now we realize that God wants to do things to us, and we must learn that his work in our souls is infinitely more important than any work of ours for him. Previously we hoped in our work, and offered him our service; now we must hope in his mercy, and learn to offer him our love. For he means to call us, like his first priests, 'not servants, but friends.'

If, then, he is leading us into the desert, it is to espouse us to himself in faith and, above all, in love. 'My son, give me thy heart!' If we are patient—for patience has indeed a perfect work—and abandon ourselves to his will in loving confidence, we shall soon find that our heart is all we have left to offer him: that love is the only gift we have for him. And at last we shall give him that gift, the only one he craves. We shall have learnt at last to understand the story of Job.

And then God will restore to us our power of serving him, but it will be a different service and a far more fruitful service. We shall be indeed 'other Christs', and our ministering will in truth be 'through him, and with him, and in him.' We shall have found 'the one thing necessary', 'the better part, which shall not be taken away.'

[1] XXI, 15
[2] Sept. 23rd 1950; A.A.S. Oct. 2nd 1950
[3] *In Joan.* 24, 4
[4] Heb. VI, 6
[5] Luke XXII, 43
[6] Ps. LXVIII, 21
[7] Cf. Luke XI, 9-13

LOVING OUR LORD

In the last chapter we referred to the need for familiar friendship with our Lord in the life of every priest, and we urged priests to pray earnestly to the Father for the gift of the Holy Spirit, that they might love our Lord as he deserves and desires to be loved. Before we discuss the unexpected aspects God's answer to this prayer may have, let us emphasize the importance of realizing that all such pleading, to be efficacious, must be based on the merits of our Lord; it must be made in the name of Jesus Christ. Moreover, its object must be such that it can fittingly be asked for in his name; the request must be in accordance with the will of the Father if our Lord is to make it his own. Generally this is where our prayers are deficient: we ask amiss. Very often our prayers are really attempts to get our own will done rather than the will of the Father.

There is, however, no doubt that the particular request we are considering—that we may love our Lord as he deserves and desires to be loved—is in accordance with the will of the Father. Such a prayer, therefore, will certainly be answered. But, as we pointed out, the nature of the answer can be quite unexpected, and quite disconcerting. And we think it is here—in our reaction to the answer—that most of us fail, and fail more than once in our lives. That we do not understand the ways of God is perhaps excusable; but that we should insist on expecting him to do things *our* way is not quite so excusable.

A type of case one very often meets is that of priests or nuns who have so far been quite successful in the work allotted to them, or adopted by them. Their labours have borne great fruit; their work is appreciated; superiors are pleased, and open in their approval; and everything seems to be going as it should. But then something starts to go wrong. Their work is not so successful as before; their superiors no longer appreciate or approve of it, and perhaps changes are made that handicap their efforts; misunderstandings arise and lead to all sorts of disappointments. They turn to God and pray confidently and earnestly—and, instead of improving, things get worse and worse the more they pray! And the result is all the more startling, and we might say the more stupefying, if they have prayed for an increase in love of our Lord rather than for the success of their work.

Time and time again one meets such a pattern of events; and time and time again one cannot help being surprised at the slowness of the persons concerned to appreciate what is really happening. Even those who are quick to understand the Divine action in other souls can be quite obtuse when there is question of God's work in their own souls. They say, like the disciples on the road to Emmaus: 'We had hoped . . .' Yes, but their hope was in plans which they themselves had made, and which they had hoped God was going to make come true, rather than in God's plans, which are often so different from ours and are *always* better and deeper and more far-sighted. They feel they could understand God's intervention if their lives had been fruitless and their work sterile—but why should he upset their successful ministry, their successful spiritual life? Yet that is precisely what our Lord has told us to expect: 'I am the true vine, and my Father is the husbandman. Every branch in me that beareth not fruit, he will take away: and every one that beareth fruit he will purge it, that it may bring forth more fruit.'[1] It is *when we are being fruitful* that he will interfere, in order that we may bring forth *more* fruit. Despite our Lord's warning, we all tend to fail in our co-operation with the Divine action at this point, and too many of us can trace our complete falling off to a persistent refusal to recognize and accept such Divine pruning.

No one who has himself made such a mistake can fail to feel sympathy for others at such a crisis, but the fact must be faced that the way of Christ is the way of the Cross, and that this must be our path too if we are to follow him. It is not only to the Jews and the Greeks that the Cross is a stumbling-block and a folly: we ourselves are not altogether free from the feeling that it should not include us. If we analysed our reactions, we would often find that we tended to think that such a way was all right for our Lord, but that *our* way should be different. Yet our Lord warned us that if we are to be his disciples we must deny ourselves, take up our cross daily and follow him. And we who are his priests, who stand daily at his altar, offering his sacrifice and identifying ourselves with him, must surely expect to be led along the road of contradiction that is the Way of the Cross.

Judged by human standards, our Lord's ministry was extraordinarily unsuccessful! When one considers the divine powers at his command, the unlimited choice he had of places, methods and instruments for his apostolate, one cannot help noting how meagre seemed the results: a handful of disciples around his Cross, most of his followers terror-stricken fugitives, and even after the crowning triumph of his resurrection, not two hundred to meet together for the coming of the Holy Spirit! Given his opportunities, *we* would certainly have done things differently! And, if the truth must be told, we still tend to do things differently. We must remember, however, that it was not by his ministry, principally or primarily, that our Lord redeemed the world, but by his Passion and Death. It was the Cross of Christ that gave us life, rather than his apostolate. And the same pattern must characterize our priesthood, which is a participation in his.

No one can or dare question the fact that every secular priest is called to active labour in Christ's vineyard. Like the Apostles, he has to minister to souls, baptizing them, instructing them and giving them the Sacraments of life. But every priest has other obligations as well, and no priest has any obligation to labour outside the limits laid down for him by lawful authority. Divine Providence may often limit a priest's activity in various ways. Illness, the orders of superiors, unsuitable circumstances are the usual ways; but God has also permitted in our time the revival, in the form of imprisonment, persecution or political pressure, the special difficulties that beset the first Apostles.

If, in one way or another, we be limited in our active apostolate, it is important to remember that other methods are at our disposal. If we go on to say that there are not only other methods but even better methods, we hope we will not be taken as being prejudiced by our own vocation in a contemplative order.

The role of contemplative orders in the work of the apostolate was underlined by Pope Pius XI when he exhorted Ordinaries in the mission field to consider the advantage of setting up monasteries of men who by their prayers and penances would water the soil of the Master's vineyard and ensure that the crop, otherwise scanty, would be made full and fruitful. We refer here to this teaching, not because we want to glorify the contemplative orders, but because we think that it implies a principle that affects every priest. For, as we understand it, the value and fruitfulness of a life of prayer and abnegation are not confined to the contemplative orders but should be shared by every priest. And, speaking *salva meliore judicio*, we feel that this was the mind of our Lord.

The text wherein our Lord replied to the disciples' comment on the readiness of the harvest for reapers, by urging them to pray to the Master of the harvest that he should send workers into the field, is often quoted in this regard; but even more important and more significant is our Lord's insistence, in his address at the last supper to his newly-ordained Apostles, on the absolute need for 'abiding' in him. We have quoted above the opening words of that section of our Lord's address. He returns to his teaching and says: 'Abide in me: and I in you. As the branch cannot bear fruit of itself unless it abide in the vine, so neither can you, unless you abide in me. I am the vine; you the branches: he that abideth in me, and I in him, the same beareth much fruit: for without me you can do nothing.'[2] One may conclude that as long as we 'abide in him', by that very fact we are doing all that is required to make our lives fruitful. It is true that no priest charged with the care of souls can claim that this principle allows him to neglect the active ministry and fulfil his obligations by prayer and private devotion. This is not 'abiding in Christ', for we cannot abide in him if we are not doing the will of his Father. When the will of the Father, shown to us by our duty, demands active work, we cannot abide in Christ without doing active work. But the important point is that even in this activity the principle of fruitfulness is our union with Christ, not the intrinsic human ingenuity or efficiency of our works.

Once we realize that union with Christ is a sufficient source of fruitfulness, we should be prepared to accept cheerfully all providential interference with the apparent fruitfulness of our ministry. We say 'apparent', because, as we conceive it, a priest is often 'bearing fruit' somewhere far removed from the place where he is, by his patient acceptance of the will of God, even when that will of God allows the immediate results of his work to diminish. And we cannot help feeling that this sort of apostolic action is more than usually common today, since such a tremendous part of the vineyard—Russia, for instance—is outside the scope of a direct apostolate. But leaving aside these personal views, we do think that every priest is called to share in our Lord's life of self-sacrifice. Our Lord sanctified himself for us. Did he not say to his Father: 'As thou hast sent me into the world, I also have sent them into the world. And for them do I sanctify myself: that they also may be sanctified in truth.'[3] Our Lord, in fact, indicates the resemblance between his own mission and that of the Apostles. His words are all the more significant in as much as they were preceded by a warning of the persecutions and the contradictions that the Apostles would undergo: 'These things I have told you, that when the hour shall come you may remember that I told you of them.'[4] It is true that not all of us are called to undergo persecution. But is it not true that all of us are called to undergo sanctification? And sanctification means pruning. The very word that expresses the principal function of our priesthood—'sacrifice'—has an implication of being made holy. Even in our work for souls, this sacrifice takes primacy of place; but in our spiritual life it must be predominant.

As priests we offer to God the sacrifice of Christ in which he is the principal Offerer and Victim. But we cannot be sincere in our offering unless we also offer ourselves with him as victim. We know that he offers us with himself. Pius XII makes that clear in the Encyclical on the Mystical Body of Christ. And Pius XI, in his Encyclical on reparation, reminds even the laity that their offering of Mass is not as it should be unless their offering of themselves and their ordering of their lives correspond in some degree to the offering and life of Christ. If this be true of all Christians, how much more clearly does it apply to us priests? There was no more ardent apostle than St. Paul, yet few have understood the mystery of the Cross, and the need for sharing in it, as he did.

Even if we were to allow our horizon to be limited by the fruitfulness of our ministry for souls, we should still be ready to renounce the satisfaction of seeing the fruit our works produce, content to know by faith that union with Christ in prayer and patience must give fruitfulness to our ministry. But we have no right to limit our horizon to such fruitfulness. The glory of God is the primary purpose of creation, and if God demands—we do not say that he does—that our lives be sacrificed with no other result but a direct glorification of himself, then we should be satisfied and feel that we have fulfilled the purpose for which we were created. God, however, has placed his glory in our fruitfulness, and we need never worry about our fruitfulness if we leave ourselves in his hands. There is no way in which we can make our lives more fruitful for God than by co-operating with his work for our sanctification.

To mention St. John of the Cross to a secular priest usually means raised eyebrows, more than mild surprise, and a general reaction of rejection. Yet the pattern traced out by St. John for the purification of the soul has its counterpart in the spiritual life of every soul that reaches the Beatific Vision. We do not say that all undergo the process to the same degree that the Saint paints in his dramatic picture of the Dark Night. Yet we have our Lord's warning to us that we must purify ourselves if we are to follow him, and we have his promise that the Father will purify us if we are to bring forth more fruit. This applies to the life of every priest. Most of us, however, greet the first touches of the divine pruning-knife with keen resentment and a lack of patience that is really quite out of harmony with the offering that we should make of ourselves each morning at Mass.

It is here—from our Mass—that our life of devotion to God might well, we think, take its daily starting point, as from a primary focus; and the Offertory of the Mass in particular is a most appropriate place for renewing our willing gift of ourselves to God and our cheerful acceptance of all that he deigns to do with us. That addition of a drop of water to the wine in the chalice, and the prayer that accompanies this ceremony, express very suitably these dispositions. It is also very suggestive that the bread and wine, after having been offered to God, are placed on the altar—a way of placing them in his hands—with the gesture of the sign of the Cross. That gesture which we make daily, first with the bread and then with the wine, should increase daily in its significance for us both as a reminder of the sacrifice that is about to take place and as an expression of our attitude before God—of our union with Christ, the Victim, and our acceptance of the Cross with him.

Then we bow down, and instead—as of old—expecting fire to come down from heaven to consume our sacrifice, we pray, with all the authority of the Church to justify us, that the Holy Ghost will come to bless our sacrifice. Now is the time to remember that our God is a consuming fire! And the fire of the Love of God which is the Holy Spirit will certainly come to sanctify us— if we do not grieve him by resisting him. But if we are going to co-operate with him we must remember the cross-marked path of our High Priest. We should be mindful, too, of the history of Job, a figure from the Old Testament too often overlooked in our time. His story is of the utmost significance for us priests, for what happened to him is going to happen to us also in some form or other. We must never forget that sanctification is not so much a question of the development and perfecting of ourselves, as of the denying of self and our replacement by Christ. We must diminish and he must increase.

Unless continual reflection on the life, the teaching and the example of our Lord has prepared us, we shall not be ready to fulfil our priestly vocation of being made men after the heart of our Lord. We must prepare ourselves to share not only his Priesthood but also his Victimhood. We have, in some way or other at least, to share in his death and resurrection. Too often our Lord has to delay his sanctifying work in our souls because of—one might say—our unbelief. And the loss of the 'more fruit' that he intended us to bring forth is not the least of the sad results of our resistance to his purifying work.

Our Lady knows the mind and the heart of Christ. Let us ask her to instruct us, to prepare us, to mould us, and to conform us to the heart of her Son, so that we may not be found unready or unwilling when he comes to ask us to ascend higher, to become more intimate with him.

[1] John XV, 1-2
[2] John XV, 4-5
[3] John XVII, 18-19
[4] John XVI, 4